Self-Esteem

Anita Naik

Illustrated by Harry Venning

*Hodder
Children's
Books*

a division of Hodder Headline Limited

For Sarah and Stephy Z – who have boundless amounts of self-esteem.

Text copyright 1998 © Anita Naik
Illustrations copyright 1998 © Harry Venning
This edition published by Hodder Children's Books in 2005

Series design by Fiona Webb

Book design by Joy Mutter

10 9 8 7 6 5 4 3 2 1

ISBN: 0 340 88395 2

Printed by Bookmarque Ltd, Croydon, Surrey

Hodder Children's Books
a division of Hodder Headline Limited
338 Euston Road
London NW1 3BH

The paper and board used in this paperback by Hodder Children's Books are natural recyclable products made from wood grown in sustainable forests. The manufacturing processes conform to the environmental regulations of the country of origin.

Contents

Introduction

My friends and I spent our teenage years in endless conversations about how we could improve ourselves, lose weight, be prettier, get boys, be more clever, get boys, be more successful and, of course, get boys. Fifteen years later and we're still talking about the same stuff. Why? Because we never found the solution to the one problem that has bugged us since adolescence – how to boost our flagging self-esteem.

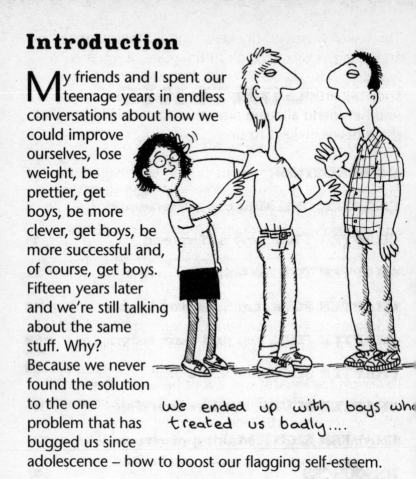

We ended up with boys who treated us badly....

We were so busy believing what everyone said about us that we forgot who we really were. More importantly, we forgot how to respect ourselves and our opinions.

Some of us were so insecure that we settled for second-best when it came to choosing careers and boyfriends. We ended up with boys who treated us badly, or boys we treated badly. A truly pathetic scene, I can tell you.

There were many in my class who let their parents and teachers dictate their future. One of my friends was desperate to be an artist, but when her father said, "All artists are losers", she gave up her dream. Another friend allowed a teacher to convince her that she'd never make it to uni.

Not everyone allows themselves to be talked out of pursuing their dreams, and for every sad story there's a happy one. One boy ignored his teacher's advice and went on to be a doctor. A girl, whose parents would not support her at drama college, is now a very successful actress.

So what makes one person achieve their dreams despite enormous set-backs, and another give up? Is it fate? Is it luck? Or is it a belief in yourself and your abilities?

I'm convinced that it's all about believing in yourself, and that's why it's so important to respect yourself. After all, until you believe in yourself you won't have the confidence to fulfil your ambitions, speak up for your beliefs, make good your dreams, and end up with the boyfriend of your choice.

Liking yourself no matter what

Everyone has moments of self-doubt, but when these overshadow everything you're in trouble. When I was 14 I had to write an essay titled: 'What I like About Myself'. Try as I might I couldn't think of one thing that I truly admired. I wasn't too happy with my looks, and my not-too-consistent marks at school left a lot to be desired (ask my mum!). I was racked with guilt about the horrible things I said to my parents, and the mean acts I played on my friends. Overall, I wasn't too impressed and spent years cheating myself of my own good company.

Now I could write that essay in a snap. It's taken 15 years to realise and, more importantly, to believe that I'm a good sort of person who does some pretty marvellous things. I still get up to mischief and I'm not convinced that I was given the right nose at birth, but I accept that the good Anita sits alongside the not-so-good Anita. And for the sake of a couple of foibles (an imperfect nose and a tendency to talk myself hoarse) I'm not going to write myself off – a girl's got her self-respect, you know. Anyway, foibles have their uses, and what may seem like a weakness may turn out to be a strength in disguise. (Do you think I could be a magazine agony aunt without the ability to talk non-stop?)

Adolescence is fraught. You feel uncertain, unsettled and unattractive. You feel as though you're in the middle of a tug-of-war – or boys we treated badly on one side is adulthood, the other childhood. One moment you're straining to grow-up, the next you're throwing your weight in the direction of childhood. On the sidelines are parents, teachers, friends, boyfriends, magazines, television programmes, films, books and advertisements which all shout messages about who you should be, what you should do, and what you should look like. Their messages often imply that you're not good enough, pretty enough or clever enough. If a girl ever needed a reason to feel bad about herself, these messages should do the trick.

Without a strong sense of self-esteem no-one can go on to fulfil their potential. There are thousands of people who keep on settling for second-best: people who are so unhappy and unfulfilled that they become prone to depression, eating disorders and self-destructive relationships.

Improving your self-esteem is the key to improving your life forever. It is your shield against the world, and your life-saver when things go wrong. Once you respect yourself, you'll know that whatever happens you'll be able to cope. Self-esteem is the ultimate confidence-giver, and the one thing that no-one can take from you.

Anita

CHAPTER ONE

What is self-esteem?

Is it (A) a self-cooking vegetable, (B) how much people like you or, (C) having a good opinion of yourself and being happy with who you are?

You have 60 seconds in which to answer, and your time starts now. Tick, tock, tick, tock etc.

I DESERVE THIS!
I DESERVE THIS!
I DESERVE THIS!

If you answered (A) or (B) you definitely need this book. If you answered (C) then you're dead clever because, yes, self-esteem is all about trusting yourself, believing in yourself and above all liking yourself. If you like yourself (even the bad bits), you'll not be passionately interested in swapping places with Britney Spears or Keira Knightley. But it's because so few of us really and truly like ourselves that I've written this book.

Many of us consistently treat one particular person unfairly, unjustly and unfavourably. In short, we're rotten to them. When this person does something embarrassing or annoying we get mad with them. When they fail, we ridicule them. We say horrid things when they look in the mirror. We hardly ever praise them. But worst of all we don't let this person be themselves and do what they want. Who is this poor person, you ask? Well, believe it or not it's you! Sometimes we are our own worst enemy.

Most of us just don't know how to be nice to ourselves. We put ourselves down for not being perfect. We hate ourselves because we're not pretty enough or skinny enough. We're hard on ourselves if we don't get top marks or are not picked for the netball team. Somehow we even manage to blame ourselves for losing a boyfriend or for not having one at all.

The only excuse (and it's not really an excuse) for being so tough on yourself is because you have low self-esteem. You have decided that you're so unimportant that it doesn't matter what you say or think about yourself. **WRONG!** And now I'm going to tell you why.

Why self-esteem is crucial

1. People achieve more when they believe in themselves.

2. Self-esteem means having the confidence to be yourself.

3. If you have self-esteem you'll respect yourself. And when you respect yourself so will everyone who knows you.

4. You'll know that it is more important to live up to your own expectations than to struggle to fulfil what others are expecting of you.

5. Self-esteem means that you don't have to prove anything to anyone.

6. You'll be much happier knowing that you're being honest with yourself.

Getting it – easier said than done

The dictionary definition of self-esteem (having a good opinion of yourself) seems simple enough but, sadly, it is easier to say than do.

Quick question:
Do you feel good about yourself?

Your automatic reply:
Sure!

But later at home when you're tearing strips off yourself for failing a test, or giving yourself a hard time for saying "Yes" when you really wanted to say "No", ask yourself the same question again. I bet your answer has changed from "Yes" to "Sometimes" or maybe even to "You've got to be kidding!"

It's not easy to treat yourself with the utmost respect, and it's very hard to listen to yourself in preference to others. But self-esteem can be relearned.

Relearned? You bet! Unfortunately, self-esteem is drummed out of most of us at an early age. We are taught that our worth doesn't come from within but from what we have, what we do, where we go, who we know and how much we are liked or disliked by others. Very rarely are we taught that it is important to love ourselves.

Measuring ourselves against these outside standards is fine when everything is going well, but what happens when things go bottom-up?

Let's say you fail an exam that everyone (teachers, parents and friends) said was crucial to your success and was, they said, so easy any fool could have passed it. Suddenly you've let everyone down (and don't they let you know it) and you've been made to look stupid. Because you're lacking self-esteem, you've allowed these unhelpful comments to make you feel worthless, depressed and insecure. You're feeling so low that you're embarrassed to face anyone who thought you would do well, and your confidence has been knocked for six.

If, on the other hand, you looked at this setback in your own terms you may not be any happier about the result, but you could rely on your own self-esteem to give you the confidence to sort it out or try again.

Self-esteem is within your grasp, if you choose to take it.

Self-esteem lets you make choices. For instance, if you are dumped by your boyfriend, you (not your friends) will decide how you are going to cope with this rejection. You may decide to mourn for weeks and become all bitter and twisted, or you may decide to say, "Well, that's life and good riddance". If looking at photographs of famous supermodels makes you feel ugly and depressed, that's your decision. A better response to the photographs would be: "I am unique in every way, so what's the point of comparing myself with anyone?" Now that's self-esteem.

There's a saying which goes like this: 'If you compare yourself with others, you may become vain and bitter. For always there will be greater and lesser persons than yourself.' You have been warned!

Vanity has nothing to do with it

"My teacher told me that only selfish people put themselves first, and that if I wanted to be liked I should help with the school play. She made me feel so bad, I stayed and helped."
Sheena, 14

"I know I'm good at maths, but whenever I mention it my friends tell me not to brag. It's almost as if they'd like me better if I was rubbish at maths, or at least pretended to be."
Laura, 17

Do you think you're attractive? If you do, I'll bet you'll never admit it. We're taught not to say positive things about ourselves. We're told not to boast, or to sing our own praises, but instead to be humble and modest.

Self-esteem has nothing to do with having a big head or thinking that you're better than anyone else. Self-esteem means believing in yourself, liking yourself, and doing what you know is right for you.

MYTH: A person who is proud of themselves is conceited.
MYTH: A person who always puts their own true needs first is selfish.
MYTH: A person who says "No" when everyone else says "Yes" is seeking attention.
MYTH: A person who thinks they are pretty is vain and conceited.

In our society any form of self-love or self-congratulation is seen as a bad thing, and labels like narcissistic (someone whose interest in themselves is over-the-top) and egotistic (someone who is unable to talk about anything but themselves) are thrown about. Do such people have self-esteem? No way. They may look confident and certain of their own opinions, but in reality they are terribly insecure people who need to prove themselves in front of others. Therefore, they spend their days trying to be the centre of attention. If they had any self-esteem they wouldn't need to prove they were beautiful, clever or important because they would know it deep-down inside themselves.

Think about the nicest person you know. Do they go around saying how great they are? Do they put you down? No, they don't. People with self-esteem don't need to talk about how they feel about themselves – they already know. They don't have to put others down in order to make themselves feel good – they already feel good.

Being the real you

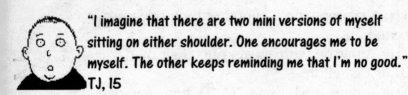

"I imagine that there are two mini versions of myself sitting on either shoulder. One encourages me to be myself. The other keeps reminding me that I'm no good."
TJ, 15

We all have different personas that we present to the world. There's the person everyone else sees – our public persona. That's the one who puts on a sweet face for their relatives, and a mean one for siblings. Then there's the person who inhabits our head, who tells us off for being mean and continually reminds us that we just aren't good enough. Finally, there is our true self. This is the one with buckets of self-esteem, and the one we desperately want to set free. Building up your self-esteem can help these three separate personas to work together instead of fighting each other. If you've got self-esteem you'll have the confidence to be yourself.

It's not a magic potion

If I've made self-esteem sound like the solution to all your problems, then that's great. But self-esteem is not a magic potion that will turn hell into heaven, or a D-grade essay into an A+ essay. Self-esteem does have its limitations.

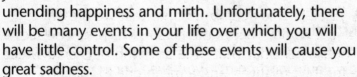

Self-esteem cannot guarantee you a life of unending happiness and mirth. Unfortunately, there will be many events in your life over which you will have little control. Some of these events will cause you great sadness.

What self-esteem can do is help you weather these storms. You will also have the confidence to move on and continue your life.

Liking yourself and believing in your own worth is the nearest you'll get to an all-over feeling of happiness.

Little Miss Nice

Getting self-esteem is not the short-cut to becoming Little Miss Nice. You'll still lose your temper with your best friend, shout at your mum, sneak on your sister and take the last chocolate biscuit in the packet. At the end of a session of being grumpy or mean you'll still be filled with guilt and remorse, but instead of pouring negative thoughts on top of negative actions, your self-esteem may help you to work out why you were so horrible in the first place.

Self-esteem won't make you an angel, but it will give you a chance to better understand yourself. You'll accept that your bad moments, just like your good ones, are an intrinsic part of your personality.

Getting a boyfriend

Feeling good about yourself will not automatically mean that you'll find Mr Right (or even Mr Almost Right), but it is fair to say that people like people who like themselves. Nobody wants to date someone who constantly needs to be told that they're loved or beautiful or clever. Having self-esteem means that you know your good points (you even know your bad points, but what the heck) and you know that you are one valuable individual. You don't need anyone to tell you. Because you respect yourself, your boyfriend will also respect you.

Proof against failure

S elf-esteem can't stop you from failing. Like happiness, failure can be beyond your control. You might not be able to even guess why a relationship went wrong, or why you failed an exam.

There's no foolproof plan against failure, but self-esteem makes for a great safety net. It allows you to take risks because you know that if you do fail, your self-esteem will let your confidence bounce back unharmed. Hate failing by all means, but never hate yourself for failing.

A perfect world

H ow many times have you berated yourself for not being perfect? If you're anything like the people I know, the chances are you do it everyday. Improving your self-esteem doesn't mean that you can make everything perfect. It just means that you will be able to accept imperfection – yours and the world's.

No matter how much we want to look like a model, we won't. This doesn't mean that you should throw your high expectations out of the window, only those which require perfection. Trying to achieve perfection is a short-cut to disaster. Self-esteem will help you accept that perfection just doesn't exist; therefore, you won't be so hard on yourself when you seem to fall short.

CHAPTER TWO

Low self-esteem?

The following list doesn't make for light, entertaining reading, and should you recognise signs of low self-esteem in yourself, don't immediately close the book because you're frightened or ashamed. Self-esteem can be learned, but before you can start to learn you've got to face up to some home truths. So keep smiling, help is just around the corner (or at least in the next chapter).

The signs of low self-esteem

• **You can't take a compliment.** Your self-esteem is so low that you can't believe that a compliment is genuine. You prefer to think that someone is playing a joke on you, or that they are disguising their pity by saying something nice.

Most likely to say: "Me? Clever! You've got to be joking!"

• **You're mean-spirited about people who you believe are prettier, cleverer or more popular than you.** You're the sort who would say nothing or, worse still, say something nasty rather than pay a compliment to someone who deserves a pat on the back. People who harbour mean thoughts or ill-will to other people are even meaner to themselves.

Most likely to say: "She's only popular because she sucks up to her friends."

• **You believe that you are so unappealing and unattractive that no half-decent guy will ever fall for you, and any who do must have something terribly wrong with them.** A word of advice: if you keep up this negative attitude, then your worst predictions will come true and you'll never get the boyfriend of your dreams.

Most likely to say: "Sam's a bit of a pain, but about all I deserve."

• **You feel that you are the only person in the whole wide world who harbours nasty thoughts.** Because you mistakenly believe that everyone else thinks only pure thoughts, you place them on a pedestal. The result: you are totally racked with guilt and shame.

Most likely to say: "I can't believe how awful I can be."

• **You stand in front of a mirror and give yourself one hell of a hard time.** Your hair is never right, your make-up's a mess, your legs are too short, and you look stupid in that dress. Why not give yourself a break and say something nice instead?

Most likely to say: "If I could just loose a few pounds I'd look loads better."

• **You don't join in a conversation because you think you have nothing to offer.** Once again you've put everyone else on a pedestal.

Most likely to think: "Why are all my friends so clever?"

• **You're afraid to take risks in case people ridicule you.** You live in constant fear of doing or saying something embarrassing.

Most likely to say: "No way am I going to make a right fool of myself in front of all these people."

• **You constantly seek the approval and opinion of others**. For example: before you choose your GCSE options, you ask all your friends what they are doing and what they think you should do. You do this because you don't value your own opinion, and even if you did, you'd keep your own ideas to yourself. You're frightened that if you take responsibility for selecting your options, it could all go wrong and then everyone would laugh. You've no idea how wrong you are!

Most likely to say: "I'd better find out what everyone else thinks first."

• **When you fail or something doesn't go according to plan, you can't forgive yourself.**

Most likely to say: "I've only got myself to blame for the trouble I'm in."

Each one of these signs means that someone is feeling very bad about themselves. They believe that they don't deserve and, therefore, won't be on the receiving end of success, love or good times. They know that their ego is so fragile that it couldn't withstand scorn or humiliation. A fall at the ice rink would totally crush them and they'd hang up their skates forever.

Think of a person you admire and secretly envy, then imagine them doing something really embarrassing. Would you think any less of them? Would you go off them? No way. Chances are that you'd laugh along with them, and admire their guts for being such a good sport.

I had a friend at school who thought she was the worst person in the world. She never answered questions in class because she was afraid that she might offer a wrong answer. She never attempted anything sporty in case she fell over. She wouldn't even talk to a boy she fancied. "He might make fun of me," she once confessed. Why was she like this? Why was she living only half a life? The answer's easy.

She believed that everyone thought she was no good. It hadn't occurred to her that she was the only one who thought this. The rest of us were too busy worrying about ourselves to keep tabs on what she was doing. It took years for her to realise that making a mistake isn't the end of the world, it's just part of human nature.

To show that you're not alone, here are extracts from letters I have received on this issue. Each one demonstrates the subtle way in which low self-esteem can affect behaviour. Read each letter and see if you can spot the writer's problem.

> "I haven't got low self-esteem. I stick up for myself and I'm not afraid to tell people where to get off. If my self-esteem was low I couldn't do any of this, could I?"
> Tina, 15

> "I don't think I'm ugly, therefore I can't have low self-esteem."
> Marie, 15

> "Low self-esteem? Not me. I have loads of boyfriends and friends."
> Sian, 16

Tina, Marie and Sian are adamant that they don't suffer from low self-esteem and, perhaps, on the face of things they don't. However, if you look behind the bravado you'll see that Sian uses a head count of her friends as a way of measuring her success as an individual. Here's the rest of Sian's letter:

> "I like having boyfriends, they make me feel wanted. I couldn't bear to be alone."

Now let's read more of Marie's and Tina's letters:

> **Marie:**
> *"My mum says that girls are either pretty or clever. My sister and most of my friends are clever, but I know I'm not. Even though I try not to let it bother me, it does."*

> **Tina:**
> *"People would walk all over me if I let them. I put them off by making it clear that I won't be messed with. I won't be anyone's doormat!"*

Marie, though confident about her looks, has no self-esteem when it comes to her abilities. She may even be using her appearance as an excuse for doing badly at school. Tina is making up for her low esteem by being aggressive. If she had any self-respect and showed it, her friends wouldn't contemplate taking advantage of her.

Like Marie, Tina and Sian, we all have our weak points which we try to protect by pretending we have self-esteem.

I have to be upfront about something: improving your self-esteem won't necessarily mean that your weak points will leave you forever. It will mean, however, that they won't become the focus of your life. No longer will one sad, bad aspect of your character cause you to dislike your whole self.

THE HOW-LOW-CAN-YOU-GO QUIZ

Still not sure if you've got a self-esteem problem? Grab a pen and a piece of paper and do this quick quiz.

1. How would your friends describe you?

a) A good listener, always helpful, never has any problems.

b) Pretty, popular and the most interesting person around.

c) Good fun, has her bad points but always apologises when she's wrong.

2. Which of the following best describes the boyfriend of your dreams?

a) Rich and devastatingly handsome.

b) Someone just like me.

c) He'll have a car that will impress my mates.

3. Do beautiful girls make you

a) Seethe with anger?

b) Feel ugly?

c) Go green with envy?

4. What do you want to do when you finish school?

a) Be a famous actress and win lots of awards.

b) Find a career or maybe go on to college.

c) Get a job. I'll take whatever's available for someone with my qualifications.

5. Your boyfriend of two months leaves you for another girl. How do you feel?
a) Mad. How dare he leave me!
b) Guilty. If only I had been a better girlfriend he would never have left me.
c) Sad, but glad to be rid of such a loser.

6. Do you have a role model?
a) Yes. She's famous and loaded with talent.
b) No. I look to myself for inspiration.
c) What's a role model?

7. Do you want to be
a) Famous?
b) Beautiful?
c) Happy?

SCORES

1. a) 0	b) 10	c) 5
2. a) 0	b) 5	c) 10
3. a) 10	b) 0	c) 5
4. a) 10	b) 5	c) 0
5. a) 10	b) 0	c) 5
6. a) 5	b) 10	c) 0
7. a) 10	b) 0	c) 5

WHAT YOUR SCORE MEANS
0-15

When it comes to self-esteem you can and do go pretty low. Being a good listener is great, but if you're always the one listening, it means you never get to talk about yourself or express your own opinions. As for always feeling guilty, at fault and inadequate (questions 4 and 6), these are also signs of low esteem. Don't worry, you can change if you want to.

20-45

Well done! You're a well-balanced person. You know that you're okay, but you also realise that upping your self-esteem is an ongoing process that becomes easier and more effective with time. Learning to respect yourself is a bit like working out. If you give up for even a month, you'll have to start from scratch again.

50-70

I can already hear you yelling "But I haven't got a self-esteem problem!" Sure, on the surface you're confident, popular and attractive. But why do you always need to impress people? Why do more attractive girls make you seethe with anger? Could it be that you don't think you're quite as good as you pretend to be?

The causes of low self-esteem

Adult put-downs

Parents are usually the first to be blamed for not boosting their children's self-esteem. In lots of instances this is a valid accusation, but in others it isn't. It's a fact that every time we step out of our front door we are putting our self-esteem on the line.

"I work in Boots on a Saturday. Last week when I couldn't find something this man wanted, he screamed at me and called me stupid. I burst into tears."
Clare, 16

To be shouted at, ridiculed or told off is demoralising no matter how much self-esteem we have. The problem with having low self-esteem in these circumstances is that you actually believe whatever was said. You trust the opinions of others more than you trust your own.

We're brought up to believe that teachers, parents and others in authority are always right. How many times have you heard people telling you to respect your elders? Respect is a good thing (and you're perfectly entitled to a fair share of respect too!), but not everything an adult recommends is likely to be in your best interests. Adults have their problems, and they sometimes act badly and believe the wrong things.

In an ideal world an adult should never put you down or be mean. An adult should never react out of anger. As we're all too aware the world is far from ideal, and sometimes you just have to go for it and make the right decisions for yourself.

Having a high sense of self-esteem will make it easier to recover from life's blows. For a start you'll know that if an adult has a go at you in any way, it's their problem not yours. You are not to blame. Really believing that you are a good person will give you the strength to shrug off the mean things people say or do.

Being compared with others

This is a guaranteed way to ruin your esteem. Boyfriends who compare you with their exes, parents who compare you with your siblings, and friends who compare you with their other friends will leave you feeling really worthless.

Bottling up your emotions

People who love us hate to see us unhappy. They will do their utmost to stop the tears and to turn a frown into a smile. They may say things like: "Don't cry, you should be happy" or "I hate to see you so upset. It's bad for you."

While their motivation is genuine, they are doing you no favour. They are teaching you to hide your true feelings. If you bottle-up your emotions and share them with no-one, you'll soon be thinking that no-one understands what you're going through. And, of course, you'll be right. How can we be understood if no-one gives us a chance to off-load our worries?

Verbal abuse

If you are told that you are stupid, ugly, fat, clumsy, and will never amount to anything, you are being verbally abused. It has been proved that verbal abuse is as harmful as other

forms of abuse. For example, if you are told often enough that you're stupid, you'll believe it and act accordingly.

Over-protected

Those who love us try to protect us from being hurt by the outside world. However, their constant protection makes you lose faith in your own ability to cope with the world beyond your bedroom door.

Suffering neglect

Neglect can be physical (for example, not being adequately fed or cared for), or it can take the form of verbal neglect where you are told that you are unwanted. If you're left with any self-esteem after such treatment, it would be a miracle.

Physical or sexual abuse

These forms of abuse totally undermine any positive feelings a person may have about themselves. Many victims of abuse end up hating themselves and feeling worthless.

Being bullied

Bullying is the quickest way of denting someone's self-esteem. Because bullies often concentrate their efforts on a single victim, the victim gets the overwhelming feeling that they have done something to arouse such hate. The victim thinks they are to blame, and therefore deserves the treatment they are getting. It's easy to see how bullying can destroy a person's ability to believe in themselves.

People we trust

One bad word from a loved one can do enormous damage to our self-respect and confidence. Because we place a lot of trust in these chosen people we believe that they wouldn't be mean to us unless we really deserved it.

High hopes

"I wanted to be perfect at everything. Once I came fourth in a dance competition, and I swore I'd never go to dance classes again. Thankfully, my mum helped me to see that my goals were unrealistic, and she told me that enjoying what I did was more important than having to win all the time."
Shannon, 16

There's nothing wrong with having high expectations, but aiming for perfection will almost certainly guarantee failure. And unless your self-esteem is as hard as a diamond, it's bound to suffer. It's far healthier to accept that you have limitations than to expect yourself to always be the best.

The slippery slope of dented self-esteem

Once your sense of self-esteem has been damaged, you'll start to feel or notice things about yourself that make you question your worth. You may begin to wonder if people really like you. For the first time ever you may even start to worry about your appearance – "I'm so ugly I'll never get a boyfriend." You may start worrying that someone will see through your defences and spot you as a fraud. To see what I mean, read Gita's letter.

> "Everyone thinks I am so talented because I've won lots of awards for playing the violin. I worry that one day they'll find out the truth. They'll see I have no talent and that luck alone has got me this far. When that happens I know they won't like me because I will have made fools of them."
> Gita, 14

Many of us with a self-esteem problem have spent sleepless nights worrying about being exposed as a fake. I promise you, it's really common. Even real-life successful women and men who have proved their skills time and again still worry that one day someone is going to tap them on the shoulder and say "You're a fraud."

It's not the exposure that's the problem. The real problem is that these people don't believe in themselves. Their self-esteem lags badly behind their talent. Why? When they were younger they may have been repeatedly told not to aim too high, or not to show off. You don't have to hear the phrase "Pride comes before a fall" too many times before you start believing it.

Non-stop activity is another sign of ebbing self-esteem. What you do is fill your day so completely that you have no time in which to think about your own well-being. Your self-esteem is so tenuous that you leave no opened windows through which self-doubt or self-interest may enter.

"I do lots of voluntary work after school, as well as baby-sitting in the evening. My parents think it's great that I am so community-minded, but I hate what I'm doing. What I really want to do is watch TV, go shopping and hang around with my friends. But I'm too afraid to give up my work. I don't want my parents to find out that I'm really selfish and lazy."
Vanessa, 16

The land of 'If only...'

Many people with low self-esteem live in the land of 'If only...': "If only my thighs were thinner, my legs were longer, my hair was blonde and my breasts were bigger then everything would be okay." It's fair enough to find something to blame when things go wrong, but you've got to make sure that you're blaming the right thing. To avoid confronting your own foibles, it's much easier to divert attention from the real problem to something else.

> "I know that if only I lived in my old town I'd be happy. I would have a boyfriend, lots of mates and heaps of things to do on the weekend. Instead, I'm stuck here in this hole and I hate it."
> Claire, 15

> "My legs are too fat. If only they were thinner then everything would be better."
> Zena, 14

Make a list of all the 'if onlys...' in your life. When you've finished take a good look at them and cross out those which are nothing more than diversions. With those remaining, which ones can you change?

For instance, if you're 5ft 2ins and want to be 6ft, then you're wishing for something that isn't possible. If your 'if onlys...' are unlikely to ever happen, it's counter-productive being unhappy about them. Throw your energy and personality behind a wish that's possible. Dreaming of 'if onlys...' rarely gets you anywhere and leaves you feeling despondent and depressed. To turn feasible 'if only...' wishes into reality, see chapter three.

CHAPTER THREE

Getting a grip

"I know I've got low self-esteem. I went to an 'Improve your self-esteem' class but it was rubbish. If you ask me, trying to learn self-esteem is a complete waste of time."
Joanna, 17

Going to classes or even reading books about improving your self-esteem is a waste of time unless you then put into practice what you've learnt. It's a bit like reading about aerobics or watching an aerobics class, but never actually doing it. Unless you're willing to sweat, you can't complain that your muscles aren't toned.

Acquiring self-esteem takes vigilance and commitment. First you've got to spot the areas of low-esteem and then commit yourself to changing them.

Upping self-esteem is not

about changing your personality. What will happen is that you will come to recognise yourself as a wonderfully worthwhile person and your outlook on life will change accordingly. But this is the important bit: the first big step is to accept that you are who you are, warts and all.

Your life is in your hands

Most of us are very good at blaming everyone and everything for the things we hate about ourselves and our lives. Instead of taking responsibility, we wrongly believe that we have no choice about what we do and who we are. We kid ourselves that we are forced into those situations which really tick us off. Nothing could be further from the truth.

For example, you feel grossly overweight and want to go on a diet, but your mum won't let you. You blame your mum for the fact that you aren't a size eight, and that loads of men aren't falling at your feet.

What you've got to realise is that you're not miserable because your mum won't let you diet, but because you're making yourself feel unattractive by dwelling on your weight. In short, you're annoyed because you feel bad about yourself!

If you had heaps of self-esteem you'd know that feeling good comes from inside, not from your dress size. Feeling good would make you want to eat sensibly, and you'd stop being off with your mum.

If you really were 'grossly overweight' your mum would be the first one to suggest that you did something about it. Agree?

Things we love to hate

Following is a list of six things that we all love to hate.

1. School: "I hate school. It's boring and I just can't bear it."
2. Appearance: "I hate being fat. It means I can't get a boyfriend."
3. Home: "I hate where I live – it's dull. There's nothing to do and no-one to do it with."
4. Money: "I hate not having any money. It means I can't do anything or go anywhere."
5. Friends: "I hate my friends. All they do is gossip, bitch and talk about boys."
6. Boyfriends: "If I had a boyfriend I'd be really happy."

Look carefully at this list and put a cross against those items over which you have no control.

SCHOOL: you may think that school is something you can do nothing about, but in reality you have absolute control. If you choose to sit in class and tune out, school is a waste of time.

What to do: decide to tune in, pass your exams, plan your future and then get the hell out of it.

APPEARANCE: you may hate your body but this doesn't mean you'll never have a boyfriend. It's more likely that your attitude is putting boys off. Take a look at couples walking down the street: very few of them have perfect bodies.

What to do: up your self-esteem by walking proud and putting a lid on negative body thoughts.

HOME: feeling bored, miserable, in a rut? Then make a decision to change your lifestyle.

What to do: up your self-esteem by triumphing over suburban hell. Set up your own club, get involved in an after-school society, or find a hobby that lets you get out and about.

MONEY: the only thing money can do is buy distractions that allow you to forget about your problems for a while.

What to do: work out just what you want money for. If it's for clothes, swap or share stuff with your mates. If it's for books and CDs – join your local library. If you think that being broke is killing your social life, ask your mates around and share the cost of renting a DVD and buying some munchies. Suddenly your social life is looking better!

FRIENDS: if you dislike what they talk about, then say so and make an effort to steer the conversation onto other topics.

What to do: up your self-esteem by mentally saying "Yes, I've got something important to contribute."

BOYFRIENDS: It's not true that finding the perfect man will make everything else okay. Relationships are tough enough without the added expectation that a boy's arm around your waist will make life sheer bliss. If you rely on a boyfriend to give you confidence, what are you going to do if the relationship fizzles out? What if he doesn't make you happy? If you think that you'll just grab another boyfriend, then you're heading for disaster.

What to do: up your self-esteem by knowing that happiness comes from within, not from whose arm you hang off.

See, you do have choices and the most important one is choosing to feel good. We can make our lives better, or we can make them a living nightmare. Having to make decisions is pretty scary. It's so much easier (and basically a cop-out) to believe that parents, teachers or friends control our lives. Have you ever considered that being in control of your life is downright empowering?

When bad things happen, your self-esteem will empower you to choose how you're going to behave. It's worthwhile remembering that while you can't always control how others will treat you, you shouldn't use that as an excuse to treat yourself badly.

Checking your behaviour

Our behaviour is always in sync with our feelings. If we feel hurt by what someone has said, we'll either fight back (for example, by saying something equally hurtful in return), or we'll take on board what they have said and go into a mood. But before you can change your behaviour (fighting back or suffering) you have to change the way you react.

For instance, someone says your new haircut stinks. Before doing anything rash, stop, think and count to three!

1. They're only telling you their opinion.

2. It's your haircut, and if you like it that's all that matters.

3. Who needs outside approval anyway? Problem solved. No need to get stressed.

It isn't always easy to spot where you're going wrong, and many of you will be trying to change the habits of a lifetime. The only way to zero in on your bad reactions is to go over old events, remember how you behaved, and then decide how you could have handled the situation better.

Learn from your mistakes

"My mum and I don't get on. Every time I get my school report she tells me my results aren't good enough. She's never told

me that she's proud of me. Her attitude
makes me so angry."
Lara, 15

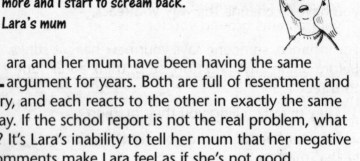

"Lara is always so defensive. Whenever I try
to point out where she's going wrong, she gets
mad at me. She screams until I can't take it any
more and I start to scream back."
Lara's mum

Lara and her mum have been having the same argument for years. Both are full of resentment and fury, and each reacts to the other in exactly the same way. If the school report is not the real problem, what is? It's Lara's inability to tell her mum that her negative comments make Lara feel as if she's not good enough. If Lara stopped screaming and used her breath to explain how she felt, there wouldn't be an argument.

Similarly, Lara's mum should have realised that praise works much better than insults.

Now that you've seen how easily one issue can be confused with another, ask yourself these questions and note down your answers on a slip of paper.

1. Think of an argument that you have time and again. What causes the argument? What's the real problem?
2. Think of a time when you took someone's constructive criticism the wrong way. How did you react? What made you react in that way?

3. Have you ever ruined a friendship? What behaviour of yours caused the break-up? What was the real reason for your behaviour?

4. What situations bring out the worst in you?

5. How do you behave when:
someone is rude to you?
someone is nice to you?
a boy asks you out?
someone takes advantage of you?
your parents ground you for a week?

Do you later come to regret how you reacted in any of these situations, and wish that you had handled them differently? If you answered 'yes' then you need to learn how to change the way you react.

For example, instead of crying when someone is rude to you, why not confront them politely about their meanness? Ask them straight out why they have to be so nasty. This a guaranteed way to embarrass a person who has a reputation for being spiteful.

If the shoe is on the other foot and you are the villain, then you have to ask yourself why you committed such a low act. What did someone do to make you behave so badly? Were you jealous? Bitter? Angry about something else entirely? Once you know what makes you act in a certain way you can go about changing it.

Full of negative beliefs

Checking your behaviour, recognising you have choices, and changing the way you react can improve your self-esteem, but sometimes the things we believe about ourselves just aren't true.

BAD EVENT → LOW SELF ESTEEM → NEGATIVE ATTITUDE → REPEAT OF BAD EVENT → LOWER SELF ESTEEM → NEGATIVE ATTITUDE → REPEAT OF BAD EVENT → LOWER SELF ESTEEM → NEGATIVE ATTITUDE → REPEAT OF BAD EVENT → LOW SELF ESTEEM → NEGATIVE ATTITUDE

Let's say that you have worked hard but keep failing maths. You now believe that you're rubbish at maths. Or maybe you've been dumped twice in a row and have convinced yourself that you're lousy at relationships. Once you start believing such negative things your self-esteem plummets, and – surprise, surprise – the bad situation will be repeated.

It goes like this: bad event → low self-esteem → negative attitude → repeat of the bad event → lower self-esteem → etc.

"I never have any luck with boys – they always two-time me. I know they're going to do it even before I go out with them. I spend all my time waiting for them to be unfaithful."
Helen, 16

It's hard to change these false beliefs – you're sort of stuck in a mental or emotional rut of your own making. If you tell yourself and everyone else that you're rubbish at maths or lousy at relationships, then you will make your own predictions come true. Your friends will come to believe that you are what you say you are. It's a nasty vicious circle.

Negative beliefs are very powerful. They can incapacitate us and make us terribly unhappy.

"My mum left my father and me when I was six years old. Whenever I was naughty my grand-mother would tell me that it was my behaviour that had driven mum away. For years I believed her and felt totally responsible for what had happened. As a result all my relationships were disastrous and I failed at everything. When I was 18 I found out that mum hadn't left because of me, but because she'd fallen in love with another man. It was as if a great weight had been lifted off me. I suddenly realised that I wasn't bad after all."
Marie, 19

True or false?

What do you think is true about yourself? On a sheet of paper write down one or two beliefs (for example, "I believe I'm a lousy daughter" or "I believe I'm selfish") that you hold about yourself, and then answer the following questions:

1. How did you come to believe this about yourself?

Who said it?
Why was it said?

If it was said by someone other than yourself, did that person have a hidden agenda? That is, did they say it because they were hurt or angry?

Did you believe this notion about yourself before someone made an issue of it?

2. Select one of your beliefs and say it to yourself. For example, "I'm fat" or "I'm stupid."

How do you feel when you say it? Do you feel as if you're repeating a lie? If you do, then that's good. Any feeling of uncertainty about what you've said is a sign that it's not a very strongly-held belief.

3. If what you said in question 2 made you feel uncomfortable, make a list of your characteristics or actions that confirm the belief. For example, if you think you're ugly list those things about your appearance that really get you down. If you can't list anything, it proves that the belief is false.

4. Now write down the things you love about yourself or that other people compliment you on. For example, your glorious mane of hair, slender fingers and bright blue eyes. Try to remember those times when you looked especially glamorous. Can't think of one? You're not trying hard enough.

The object of that exercise was to show you that there are negative and positive experiences that can be used to support or crush the things that we believe about ourselves. It's your decision – not anyone else's – whether you choose to believe the bad or the good about yourself.

Find a role model

I mproving your self-esteem can be hard and lonely, so why don't you find a worthwhile ally – a role model – to help? A role model is someone you admire.
What you should know about your role model:

• How did they get to where they are now?

• What obstacles did they overcome?

• What mistakes have they made?

• How did they handle their mistakes?

• How do you think they would react when someone is nasty to them?

• What is it about your role model that makes you feel good?

"My teacher is a great role model because she encourages me and never puts me down."
Tina, 14

"I would choose J.K. Rowling as my role model because everyone told her she couldn't write and would never be a successful author. She refused to believe them and look where she is now."
Seema, 15

"My sister is my role model because she is the most genuine person I know."
Karen, 15

"I want the writers Paula Danziger and Judy Blume on my self-esteem team because their books show that it's fine to be yourself."
Leah, 13

Who is your role model? A supermodel? An actress? A writer? Your mum? A friend? Why do you like them? Is it because they are pretty, rich and lead a glamorous life? If it is, then you may like to re-think your choice. There's nothing wrong with liking someone for these reasons, but the job of a role model is to help you learn something about yourself.

Job specifications for a role model

- They're not perfect, but human and acknowledge that they have flaws.

- They're big-hearted people with a generous and positive spirit.

- They make you feel good about yourself and your potential.

- They don't put anyone down.

- Their self-esteem is not based on their success.

- They can laugh when things go wrong.

- You trust them, but they give you the gumption to trust yourself even more.

CHAPTER FOUR

Love, sex and boys

We are all very vulnerable when it comes to forming relationships. In the arena of love our insecurities are under the spotlight for all to see. Who hasn't felt the humiliation of rejection or the pain of being dumped? Who doesn't understand the heartbreak of being told to get lost and the loneliness of being single? Who can honestly say, with hand on heart, that relationships aren't a problem?

Bad relationships happen for all sorts of reasons. Sometimes one partner can be blamed. In other instances the breakdown is the fault of both parties or even a third party. The single most important point to accept about a break-up is this: low self-esteem hinders relationships. It makes troublesome ones worse, and causes good ones to crumble. If you're single, low self-esteem causes you to keep prospective boyfriends at arm's length.

"I stayed with Gary even though he two-timed me. I was so glad to be going out with someone, that I forgave him everything."
Rachel, 15

"I always fancy boys who wouldn't look twice at me. When a boy does like me, I automatically think they're weird and write them off!"
Anna, 16

"My boyfriend slaps me now and then. It's usually my fault for nagging him."
Nina, 15

"I know exactly why I haven't got a boyfriend. It's because I'm a really horrible type of person."
Chrissie, 16

"When boys ask me out I say 'yes' straight away. I don't even bother to consider whether I like them or not."
Sue, 14

Five girls, five examples of low self-esteem. These girls feel that they have nothing to offer a boy. They don't like themselves, they don't believe in themselves and above all they don't respect themselves. They put up with being treated appallingly because they don't believe they are worth being treated well.

High self-esteem will not solve all your relationship problems, nor will it help you find the man of your dreams, but it will stop you from tolerating anything less than the best. It will also help you to:

- Like and love yourself more – now that's got to be healthy.

- Not be taken advantage of.

- Get out of bad relationships.

- Not mistake sex for love.

- Understand that romantic crushes have nothing to do with real love.

Romance vs. love

Do you think that boyfriends are the key to happiness? Not sure? See if you are guilty of any of the following:

- Do you think that your life would be perfect if only you were in love?

- Do you believe that there is only one real love for you?

- Do you assume there's something wrong with you because you're single?

- Do you go out with the first Tom, Dick or Harry who asks?

- Are you postponing making decisions about your future in case Mr Right comes along?

- Are you waiting to be 'saved' by someone?

- Do you believe in love at first sight?

- When you're not in love are you unhappy?

- Do you only feel complete when you've got a boyfriend?

- To get a boy to fancy you, do you play up those aspects of your personality that you know he likes?

- Does loving someone mean owning them?

If you responded with a 'yes' to one or more of these questions, then you're one of life's great romantics. This doesn't mean you're into flowers, candlelight and love songs, but you are in love with the notion of being in love.

Romantics often lack faith in themselves, and instead

of accepting that life will be as good as they make it, they wait for Mr Right to make it good. One good-looking man on their arm, and they think life will be great.

They also have illusions about the nature of love and what it means to be in a relationship. They are prone to having crushes, and their romantic beliefs often lead them to fall in love with any boy who passes.

Above all, romantics rarely trust their own instincts about people or relationships. They are so caught up in romantic ideals that they don't realise that what they are doing is avoiding real love. This is why their relationships never amount to much or never even happen at all.

To stop forming dead-end relationships or to get out of horrid ones, you'll have to swap your bad love attitude for a good one. Try the following four-point plan to improve your outlook on love.

POINT 1: Boyfriends are not the solution to your problems.

There is no Prince Charming who will come to your rescue, save you from your so-called life and make you Princess Happiness. There is only one person who can, and that's you! So go for it!

> **BAD FACT:** Going out with a good-looking guy won't make you feel more attractive, just more insecure about your own looks.
> **BAD FACT:** Going out with a confident guy won't make you lose your shyness. On the contrary,

you'll become more aware of it.

GOOD FACT: There are boys you can have a good time with and still be yourself.

GOOD FACT: The quality of your life is determined by you.

POINT 2: Boys like girls who like themselves.

No-one wants to date someone who hates the way they look, is unable to accept a compliment graciously, is constantly looking for reassurance, and feels insecure about their relationship.

"My last girlfriend was obsessed with dieting and was always asking me if I thought she was fat. When we broke up she was convinced it was because of her figure. It wasn't. I was just bored with her fixation about her weight."
Tom, 17

"Why are girls so insecure? They always want to know if you love them, if you still like them, if anything is wrong, if they look nice, what they've done to upset you and why you're going out with your mates instead of them. I just don't understand where girls are coming from."
Mark, 16

POINT 3: Don't put your life on hold in the name of love.

There are lots of girls who wait for a boyfriend to come onto the scene and make their lives complete.

They are deep into the "if only . . ." syndrome:
"If only I was in love, then I wouldn't feel lonely, sad, and bored."

> **BAD FACT:** If your expectations of a relationship are so high, what's going to happen if your boyfriend leaves you?
>
> **GOOD FACT:** If you can be happy on your own, then your relationships are much more likely to be happy ones as well.

POINT 4: Don't be fooled into thinking you're not complete without a boyfriend.

The two best things that you can bring to a relationship are: yourself (the real one), and the confidence of knowing that you are one happy person whether you have a boyfriend or not. If you are self-reliant, then insecurity flies out the window.

> **GOOD FACT:** Boyfriends are great, but they aren't the be-all and end-all.
>
> **GOOD FACT:** If you concentrate on leading a full life with interests of your own and friends you can rely on, you're more likely to end up with good relationships.

Singledom

So you're single – what does this mean to you? Sad, lonely loser who no-one wants? Or normal person who just hasn't found someone she wants to date yet? Mmm...chances are you wanted to pick the second

choice but inside the first one felt more real. Well, if it did, don't despair because most single people, no matter how old or what sex they are, go through pangs of "no-one wants me" or "what's wrong with me?". Everyone sometimes feels lonely and would rather be with someone else. However, if you feel like that all the time you need a wake-up call. Having a boyfriend doesn't make you a better

person, more attractive, or even clever. It won't take away low self esteem and it won't make you happy if you can't be happy on your own. Would you want to date someone who felt down on themselves and constantly needed you in order to feel good? Of course not! So don't fall into the single self-pity trap. Sure you haven't got a boyfriend at the moment but (1) It's not the end of the world, (2) It doesn't mean you never will have one and (3) Think how fun the search will be until you get one!

Why do you want a boyfriend?

1. "Because my friends have one." (Your friends also have zits, nightmares, bad breath, and allergies to cats. Do you want those as well?)

2. "I won't be bored at the weekend. I'll have a social life." (You don't need a boyfriend, you need to get out there and enjoy some time with your friends!)

3. "I won't be humiliated on Valentine's Day." (Ah, now there's a solid basis for forming a deep and meaningful relationship, I think not.)

4. "It will make me feel attractive." (How?)

5. "All girls are supposed to have boyfriends." (Oh, yeah? Who said?)

These are five very common reasons for a stint of boyfriend-hunting. Do you want to hear a great reason for dating the boy in Year 10? Well, here it is: "I've met someone I really like."

Until you can say these six simple words and mean them, then what's so wrong with being single? Being single doesn't mean you're unattractive, and it certainly doesn't mean that you'll never fall in love.

What do boys want?

We're often led to believe that boys don't like 'their girls' to behave in certain ways or to excel at certain things. That's why many girls hide who they really are in the hope that a boy will like them. Behaving like a chameleon to ensnare your man is bad news. It's exhausting and demoralising having to pretend.

GOOD FACT: If someone doesn't like you for who you are, then they're not the right person for you.

My friends and I have done some pretty dumb things to make boys like us. One pretended she was into Russian films, and then had to endure countless Saturday nights watching black-and-white Russian videos. Fine if you're really into that stuff, incredibly boring if you're not. Another went bungee jumping even though she was afraid of heights. She decided she would rather risk her neck for this guy, than own up to her fears. Me? I was good at toning down my ideas and beliefs, and would keep quiet even when my boyfriend said the most outrageous (and often offensive) things. All that selling-out just to impress. But what's so impressive about pretending to be someone else? Isn't it the same as lying?

We often get this boyfriend thing wrong because our 'belief system' is screwed up. What we believe to be true about 'what boys like' is often totally false. Over the years I have received hundreds of letters from girls telling me what they think boys like. It doesn't take a genius to look down this list and to realise that something is not quite right.

Boys don't like girls who:

talk too much
don't talk
eat too much
are worried about their weight

are loud
are too shy
sleep around
are frigid
are too short/flat-chested/have hairy legs
are too tall/big-chested/artificial
are clever
are stupid

Other than the fact that the items contradict each other, would you judge your best friend according to this list? Would you hate her because she talks a lot? Or put her down because she's big-chested? No, of course you wouldn't. Would you be put off by a boy because he's great at sports or is not too clever? No. You like your friends because they are who they are; they don't play hide-the-real-me games.

Imagine how you'd feel if you found out that your best friend had been feigning an interest in, say, horses just so that you would like her. My guess is that you'd be pretty disgusted. You'd think her weak and characterless.

Let's apply the same rule to boys. How would your boyfriend feel when he realised that he'd been dating a pretender? Duped, maybe?

Forget turning personality somersaults to impress. Instead, show that you're proud, happy and delighted to be you. It also helps if you show that you're proud when someone else is being their truly adorable self.

The one-sided crush

"I've never had a boyfriend but I've had loads of crushes. They feel like real love and make me happy except for one thing – they're lonely."
Laura, 15

"I have crushes to avoid being rejected."
Paula, 16

Crushes are often the first step on the stairway of love. They are a safe way of learning how to deal with all the ups and downs of a relationship.

Some girls never have crushes, others have a new one every week. If you happen to constantly have a crush on someone, don't worry. There's nothing wrong with you, and when you're ready to have a relationship you will.

The big drawback with crushes is, of course, that they are one-sided. You choose the object of your passion, pick the story line, and direct all the action. (Like you decide how the relationship develops and even dies.) In your mind you create scenes where your man strays but returns because you are the one he truly loves. You also credit your crush-love with fame, brains, kindness and general gorgeousness. It's great to have the occasional fantasy, but don't confuse it with the real thing. If you set out to find the perfect made-in-heaven relationship, you're really just avoiding true-life relationships. Remember: perfection in anything does not exist.

> "I don't like any of the boys I know. There's always something wrong with them. They dress badly, like naff music or have strange habits. I really fancied this one guy until my friend pointed out that he had a big nose. I soon went off him. That's why I'm better off sticking to my pop-star crushes – they never do anything to put me off."
> Sophie, 15

Dismissing all the boys you know because they're not perfect is a reflection on yourself. When you don't like yourself, it's easy to find fault with others.

When you can accept your own flaws as being 'normal', then you're able to accept the flaws of others.

Though your pop-star or film-hero crush may seem perfect, he isn't. What you see at the cinema and read in the press is a manufactured product that never lets you suspect that your heroes are loaded down with human-type flaws. Yep, celebs can be mean and nasty, have odd habits and do unsavoury things. Oh, and by the way, your crush may also have some serious work to do on their own self-esteem.

Saying "I love you"

"My boyfriend won't tell me he loves me. If he really cared for me he would, wouldn't he? He seems to like me, but he won't take it further than that. Is there something wrong?"
Helen, 16

"I don't know why, but I can't tell my boyfriend I love him. I try but it just gets caught in my throat."
Sue, 14

Getting worked up by these three little words is bad news. 'Love' is an over-used and much-abused word. Many say it without meaning it. If you want to know how your boyfriend feels about you, then look at the way he treats you.

Does he respect you?
Does he encourage you to do your best?
Does he make you laugh?
Does he show consideration for your needs?

The answers to these questions will help you to see whether or not he loves you. Let's face it, it's far better to judge someone by their deeds than by what they say.

If you can't bring yourself to say "I love you" it may be because you're uncertain about your feelings, or too embarrassed to be so frank. You may also be afraid that your honesty will be thrown back in your face and you'll be a laughing stock. Oh, this love business can be a nightmare.

Saying "I love you" and meaning it takes courage. The implications are huge and frightening. But before you can say it to others, you have to be able to say it to yourself.

Do you love yourself?

Do you respect yourself?

Can you forgive yourself when you make mistakes?

If you responded 'yes' each time, then you'll have no problem sharing your love with someone when the time is right.

Sex and love — they're not the same

"I don't want to sleep with my boyfriend, but I feel he'll leave me if I don't."
Sue, 15

"I really want to be in love – it just never happens. I sleep with loads of guys, but it never turns into a proper relationship. In fact, they don't want anything to do with me later."
Lorna, 16

Double standards stink! Ever heard of a boy being called a slut, easy or cheap? How often have you passed away an afternoon with your girlfriends slagging off a guy for being frigid? Never. So why do girls get all this grief? It beats me, but the unfairness of it all makes me really annoyed.

Sex – doing it or not doing it – is used to batter your self-esteem. If you do it too much, you're a slut; if you don't do it at all, you're frigid. It's a no-win situation. The only thing you can do is ignore what people say.

The truth is there is no such thing as being frigid or a slut. Some girls sleep with lots of boys, some girls don't. As long as you alone have made the decision about whether to have sex or not to have sex, then you have only yourself to answer to. Time to drag in a bit of Shakespeare: "This above all: to thine own self be true."

Sexual don'ts

- Don't let anyone tell you that sex is a must in a relationship. It isn't.

- Don't have sex unless you feel ready, and you really want to do it.

- Don't have sex simply because everyone else is doing it.

- Don't do it just because you're 16, legally entitled and can't think of a reason why you shouldn't.

- Don't do it to save a relationship.

- Don't confuse having sex with being in love.
  If you think that having sex with your partner will automatically lead to a love relationship, you've got to think again. You are making one big mistake.

Sex is a physical act and unless there was emotional commitment to begin with, emotional fulfilment will not follow. If you're having sex in the hope that it will make you feel more attractive or wanted, then you're having sex for the wrong reasons.

The only thing that is 100 percent guaranteed to make you feel attractive and loved is having high self-esteem. Not only will it empower you to make life choices that are right for you, it will also help you to understand why you're making those decisions.

Coping with rejection

Many of us take rejection to mean that we're not good enough. We think it is because of our 'faults' that the relationship is on the rocks.

"For months after the break up I kept asking myself what I had done to make it go all wrong. What sort of person should I have been to make everything okay? Is there something wrong with me? Maybe I'll get it right next time."
Liz, 15

Relationships end for any number of reasons, and it's rarely the fault of only one person. Love doesn't always last forever, and the fatality rate for first love is very high. If you've been ditched, don't take it as a sign that you're lacking in something. If the relationship was an honest one where you were being true to yourself and to your boyfriend, then remember that you're still that same wonderful person that he wanted to date originally. You haven't changed, the chances are that he has.

So stop torturing your self-esteem with a whole heap of 'if onlys...': "If only I had been prettier," "If only I had worn the red dress and not the baggy trousers." If only you could stop needlessly blaming yourself you might be able to lead a proper life!

Being rejected is painful. It knocks your confidence, makes you feel worthless and, if you let it, it can take over your life. Don't imagine for one minute that this relationship was your first and last, because it won't be. If you can't get your heart around that fact, then open your mind to this one: everyone finds their special someone in the end.

Boyfriends who hit and shout

"My boyfriend calls me bad names and sometimes hits me. I put up with it because I love him, and I know that it is caused by something I've done. He's always so sorry afterwards. I know he means it."
Remy, 16

Girls stay with boys who abuse them for all kinds of reasons: they're frightened of a retaliatory beating, they're scared of being alone, or even because they think they deserve it.

Verbal bullying or physical abuse destroys self-esteem. It makes the innocent victim feel humiliated and ashamed and therefore too afraid to do anything about it.

If you're being abused tell someone what's going on and get help as soon as possible. Contact Childline on Freephone 0800 1111, or tell your parents, a trusted adult, the school counsellor, a teacher or the police. And do it now before you are seriously hurt!

Giving boys a hard time

"People tell me I treat my boyfriends badly. My answer to them is: 'So what if I do?' It sure beats letting my boyfriends do it to me. I once had a boyfriend I was nice to, but he walked all over me. I've got it sussed now and that will never happen again. Treat them mean, keep them keen."
Lou, 16

Someone treating you badly is no excuse for treating others the same way. There are two courses of action open to you if someone doesn't treat you right.

Number one: see it as their failing and walk away with your head held high.

Number two: blame yourself for letting it happen and then build a shield round yourself to make sure it never happens again.

Number two is a really bad option. First, you attack your own self-esteem. Second, the shield will also keep out good relationships.

FACT TO REMEMBER:

There is never a good excuse to hit or to yell abuse at anyone.

There is no excuse for treating boyfriends (or anyone for that matter) badly. You should always treat others the way you expect to be treated. If you're being mean to someone, you'd better check out your motives – they definitely need an overhaul.

If you let rip at your boyfriend, ask yourself the following questions. They may give you an insight as to what's really getting to you.

- Are you mad about something else but are unable to talk about it honestly?

- Are you too afraid to end the relationship and hope that your bad behaviour will lead your boyfriend to do it?

- Are you lashing out because you think this is the way people in love behave?

- Are you letting your boyfriend know that he and this relationship don't live up to your expectations?

- Are you seeking attention? If so, why?

- Are you testing him and the strength of your relationship by showing him your worst side? (This strategy is bound to backfire, so don't use it.)

These warning signals are telling you that it's time to talk to your boyfriend. If your relationship is worth anything, it's worth five minutes of honest, upfront discussion. The longer you hold your feelings inside, the worse the whole thing will become.

There are no guarantees of a happy ending, and if the differences are too big to overcome, then accept that you (and him) will be better off breaking up.

CHAPTER FIVE

You and your body

When I started writing this chapter I did a quick straw poll among my friends to find out what they thought about their bodies. Their responses were: "I hate all of it," "It's ugly," "I need to lose weight," "I'm too thin," "I'm all lumpy," "I hate my freckles," and "My hair frizzes in the rain." Not only didn't they have anything positive to say, but all of them gave me their answers in a flash. Their responses were so quick it gave me the impression that my friends spent a lot of time thinking about their bodies.

I then contacted some other friends and asked them what they love about their bodies. I told them that things like personality, clothes, jewellery and make-up didn't count. There were some very long silences before my friends came up with answers. Sadly, some couldn't think of anything they loved, some begrudgingly said that they had seen worse, but only a handful had something flattering to say.

Most of us excel at saying mean things about our bodies. We always focus on the bits we hate. We totally overlook the fact that we have good bits as well. If we say negative things often enough we really start to believe them and, in turn, find it even harder to say something in praise.

We also make a start in the cover-up business. For example, instead of saying outright that we hate our bodies, we say "Oh well, it's personality that counts". True enough for sure, but how we feel about our bodies is tied up with our personalities. You can't separate them no matter how hard you try.

Seeing your body as a positive force will improve your outlook, and how you respond to people. Until you learn to respect your body as much as your mind, behaviour and attitudes, you will never wholly respect yourself.

Love me, love my body: the benefits

1. You'll glow with inner confidence. You'll feel good about yourself, accepting that even the most perfect looking people have flaws.

2. You'll know that you're unique, and will, therefore, save loads of time and angst by not comparing yourself to anyone (especially supermodels).

3. You'll be saying bye-bye to bad hair days. No longer will zits or unruly hair rule your mood, turning potential good times into nightmares.

4. You'll no longer give your friends the hard once-over. By accepting that everyone is unique and by being proud of yourself, you will stop being Little Miss Critical.

5. You'll be more comfortable when going out. For a start you won't hide behind chairs worrying that someone will notice your thick ankles. Instead, you'll be mingling with your friends and enjoying a good laugh.

6. Get-thin fads will pass you by. Your body is a temple so you'll do nothing to harm it.

7. Words will never hurt you. Those nasty and uncaring comments that once upon a time would have made you cry for a week will no longer bother you. But because you're a level-headed person you'll accept fair criticism when you recognise it's for your own good.

What causes an image problem?

A bad self-image can be brought about in lots of different ways and under the influence of key people in our lives (for example: parents, friends and

boyfriends). It can also be caused by those whose main interest is self-interest (for example: the media and the diet industry).

Parents

Does your mum always criticise the way she herself looks? Does she go on diets and wish she was more attractive? If she does, the chances of you also suffering a self-image problem are high.

"My mum is always dieting. I can't remember a time when she didn't eat cottage cheese for dinner. My dad, on the other hand, eats loads, is quite fat and doesn't seem bothered by his build. I once asked my mum why she gets so carried away, and all she said was that it's a woman's duty to be slim."
Sara, 14

> "My grandmother used to call my mother 'Fatty' when she
> was a child, and now my mum diets all the time. You'd think
> that my mum's experience would mean that she would treat
> me differently, but she doesn't. She is always saying that
> boys won't like me if I'm too fat."
> Tina, 15

If your mum, or even your dad, makes you feel bad
about your body, then it's time to talk. Bullying
tactics, no matter how genuine the concern, never
work. They destroy self-esteem, often to a point
where you seek comfort by further indulging in those
things you are being warned off. Tell your parents to
stop the bullying now.

Friends

Without realising it friends can make you feel bad
about the way you look. They may offer bad
advice or repeat uninformed opinions.

Sometimes bad vibes spread like ripples on the surface
of a lake. One friend starts putting herself down, and
before you know it the whole group finds something to
gripe about. For many girls a conversation is nothing
more than an exchange of self-directed unpleasantries.

> "My friends make fun of my breasts because they are big.
> They call me 'Miss Page Three', and I hate it. I don't think
> it's funny and I want to die when they say it. I laugh with
> them because I don't want them to think I'm a spoil-sport."
> Tracy, 15

If you've had an experience similar to Tracy's then it's time for you to pull out all the stops and become assertive. If you don't like being called names (even if it is meant in harmless jest), speak out. Laughing along with your friends only gives them an excuse to tease you again and again. There's no need to get heavy, simply say that their comments really hurt your feelings.

While it can be hard for you to cope with the nastiness of your peers, it is an equally hard slog for your friends to keep bolstering your confidence. If you're always asking your mates what they think about your looks, your hair, your clothes etc, you're doing nothing more than manipulating your friends. You're fishing for compliments to help bolster your flagging self-image.

The only advice I can offer is this: don't do it. You're further weakening your self-esteem (if you've got to ask others for their opinion, it means you don't value your own) and annoying your mates.

Do yourself a big favour and learn to trust yourself. If you think you look good, that's all you need.

Boyfriends

Boyfriends can be a menace to our self-esteem. One friend was told she had a 'huge butt' by her boyfriend. Even though he took it back immediately and said it was only a joke, she never got over it. Ten years later and she still refuses to go onto the beach without wearing a long T-shirt. The truth is she has the smallest bottom in the world, but she is determined not to believe what she sees in the mirror. She prefers to run (ruin, more like it) her life on the basis of one careless comment.

"My boyfriend wants me to dye my hair, use more make-up and wear sexier clothes. Doesn't he like me the way I am? Am I that gross?"
Liz, 15

If your boyfriend isn't happy with the way you are, then tell him you're not happy with his attitude. The people who are worth hanging onto are those who accept you the way you are.

To be fair, some girlfriends have to smarten up their act as well. It's equally demoralising for a boyfriend to see you lusting over male models with washboard stomachs and bulging pecs.

The media

Television, magazines, and films have a lot to answer for when it comes to inflicting damage on our self-esteem. On one hand they establish 'role models' (for example, supermodels with flawless skin and split-end free hair), and on the other hand make banner headlines (for example, 'Skinny models make girls anorexic') out of our apparent misery.

Let's give ourselves a break and give credit where credit's due. Most of us know that we're never going to look like a supermodel, and are not so foolish as to attempt serious malnutrition in order to look like a pencil.

However, what most of us do instead is compare ourselves to supermodels until we feel thoroughly disappointed and despondent. For instance, we see a photograph of a beautiful actress or model and we look at her skin, hair, sexy clothes and then look at our reflection and say "Aaaargh!!!". So the problem lies not with the model, but with the comparison we choose to make. Let's look critically at our supposed super 'role' models.

1. Their skin looks flawless because their photographs are touched up to remove any blemishes.

2. They look stunning because they spend three hours in make-up and two hours having their hair done before a photography session.

3. They look sexy because they are wearing a zillion pounds worth of designer clothes on their back.

4. Photographers shoot rolls and rolls of film just to get one perfect shot.

5. Glam lifestyles, beauty and success have nothing to do with being happy and full of self-esteem.

I don't know about you, but when I look at points 1 to 5, I truly believe that I too could be catwalk material given all the help that supermodels get. The problem is, I'm not interested in borrowing an image, I want my own.

The get-thin business

The diet industry is worth over £1 billion pounds a year in the U.K. alone. With this much money at stake, do you really think that the manufacturers of diet products are concerned with how you feel about yourself? The short answer is: no way. Even though many of us are sceptical about this whole business, we are still a nation obsessed with dieting. Run your eyes down these statistics:

- 1.7 million people in Britain say that they are 'constantly' on a diet.

- 200,000 women and female adolescents in the UK have an eating disorder.

- There are currently over 300,000 books about dieting on sale in the UK.

Now, compare those statistics to the following:

- 98 percent of women estimate their body size to be 25 percent larger than it really is.

- 50 percent of women regain weight lost through dieting.

- Women are far more likely to be underweight than men.

- 1 in 5 children in Britain are overweight and 1 in 10 are obese.

The problem with many diet plans or manufactured calorie-controlled foods is that they don't help you to modify your eating practices. In other words, they don't help you to find out why you wolf down five Mars Bars and three packets of crisps on the trot. So at the end of a diet regime, you immediately go back to your old eating habits.

Diet plans also make a big song and dance about eating only 'good' food, therefore leaving you with terrible cravings for the 'bad' stuff. And human nature being what it is, you immediately break your diet and eat the banned goodies. You then put on weight, feel a failure because you can't stick to your diet, and seek comfort in food. An awful cycle when you think about it.

If you're sure you really need to lose or gain weight, go and see your G.P. Ignore the miracle cures (there aren't any) and the advice of friends and family. And above all don't become a victim of media or fashion hype. Your doctor alone knows the true score, and he or she will be only too happy to give you sound advice.

If you have an eating disorder please seek professional help. A good place to start is:

The Eating Disorders Association,
103 Prince of Wales Road, Norwich, Norfolk, NR1 1DW
www.edauk.com
Tel: 0845 6347 650

Mirror, mirror on the wall...

Some people find looking in a mirror a complete nightmare. Others run a mile at the mere mention of having their photograph taken. For these people their body gives them no pleasure, but heaps of pain.

Imagine having to look the other way every time you saw a mirror or glimpsed a snapshot, just so that you wouldn't be reminded of how bad you look. This is one unhappy soul who can never find her best side, can never take a compliment and yet stores up all the negative things people say so that she can remind herself of them constantly.

If you recognise aspects of yourself here it's time to start working on your self-image. Jot your answers (a,b or c) on a piece of paper and tally up your score at the end.

THE ULTIMATE IMAGE TEST

1. When you walk past a mirror do you
a) Glance at your reflection?
b) Look the other way so that you don't catch sight of yourself?
c) Stop and check out how you look?

2. How often do you weigh yourself?
a) Never – it would be too frightening.
b) Every day.
c) Now and then.

3. What word would you take to be the biggest insult?
a) Stupid
b) Fat
c) Ugly

4. Which of the following fills you with dread?
a) Walking around in your underwear in front of your friends.
b) Playing sport in front of a crowd of male onlookers.
c) Being seen without make-up.

5. If you had one wish what would it be?
a) That everyone found you attractive.
b) That you were someone else.
c) That your thighs were thinner, your hair longer and your nose smaller.

6. As you walk past two boys you hear them laugh. What do you think they are laughing at?
a) You and how you look.
b) A stupid joke.
c) They are probably embarrassed because they fancy you.

7. It's your best friend's birthday party tonight, and nothing you do or wear makes you feel good or look pretty. Do you go to the party?
a) Yes, but hide in the shadows all night.
b) No. It'll only make you depressed for the next fortnight.
c) No way! You never go out unless you look and feel absolutely wonderful.

8. How would your friends describe you?
a) Immaculately turned-out – always!
b) Dumpy, but with a great personality.
c) Cheerful, and sort of scruffy. Only wears clothes that make her feel really comfortable.

Scores

	a	b	c
1.	a 5	b 0	c 10
2.	a 0	b 10	c 5
3.	a 5	b 0	c 10
4.	a 0	b 5	c 10
5.	a 10	b 0	c 5
6.	a 0	b 5	c 10
7.	a 5	b 0	c 10
8.	a 10	b 0	c 5

WHAT YOUR SCORE MEANS

0-20

You bear the classic traits of someone who has low self-esteem and bad self-image. Because you are so preoccupied with how you look, you assume that everyone else is as well. Does the word paranoid mean anything to you? But fret not, the do-it-yourself image kit is only a page away.

25-55

You're doing pretty well in the image stakes. You know that you're not perfect (and we all know that no-one is), and that you have off days and on days. Read on to find out about banishing the off days for good.

60-80

On the surface you seem to literally bubble over with self-esteem on the image front, but could it be that you're hiding the real you under make-up and smart clothes? Not sure, then keep reading.

What you can do for your self-image TODAY!

The first step in dealing with a low self-image is to realise that there are things you can change and things you can't.

Draw up a large piece of paper into five columns and head the first three columns with these headings: 'Things I hate about my body', 'Things I can change', and 'Things I can't change'. Fill in the first column and tick whether it is something that can or can't be altered. If you hate your weight, then that is something you can change. If you hate the fact you're very short, that's something you can't alter.

Remember when we were talking about diets and we said that diet plans don't help you to understand what compels you to pig-out, well the same applies in this situation. You have to know why you want to change.

So in column four write down your reasons for wanting to make changes. For example, 'I want to be fit and healthy because I'm tired of feeling flabby and lazy.'

That's a perfectly sound reason. But if you had said that you were doing it to impress your boyfriend, you'd be on the wrong track and wasting your time. Firstly, you're only pretending to make a change, and will most probably go through another make-over to suit the requirements of your next boyfriend. Secondly, you can't change other people. Your sudden transformation into a weekend health-freak won't change your boyfriend's opinion of you. Like I said, a waste of time and, in this case, sweat.

Real change comes from within and affects you before it influences those around you. Making yourself fitter, more confident and more assertive will make you a happier person, and you never know who you might meet in the gym.

Mark column five with the heading 'Taking action'. Under this heading you can suggest ways of dealing with the changeables. For example: if you want to lose weight, in the action column you could write 'Reduce junk food, eat more fruit, and go swimming twice a week.'

If you're not sure how to implement change in areas like shyness or assertiveness, check out your local library for courses or seek the advice of the school counsellor or other trusted adults. Library shelves groan under the weight of self-help books. Some are extremely useful, others not, so try to get a recommendation before relying on their advice.

Whatever action plan you design, work on it at your own pace. Don't listen to the well-meaning, but often self-serving advice of friends or family. By all means practise the advice of professionals like doctors, dieticians, or sports instructors. If you make a decision to change something you dislike, remember the following:

- It won't make all your other problems disappear.

- It won't happen overnight.

- If your plan doesn't work first time, try again.

- Working toward your goal at your own pace is more likely to end in success.

The unchangeables

Those things which can't be changed are a fundamental part of you. You can choose to accept them, or choose to let them get you down. (No prizes for guessing which is the better idea.) Acceptance won't mean that you'll become instantly and blissfully happy, but it will mean that you can stop blaming the unchangeables for all your misfortunes. Is it really logical to blame your freckles for not getting picked for netball, for not getting the female lead in *Romeo and Juliet* and for having boring weekends?

"You don't know how horrible it is to have pale skin. I look terrible in summer and have to wear trousers to hide my white legs. I wish more than anything that I could tan. I know I'd look much better with glowing olive skin. I'm tired of hiding away all summer by myself."

Carla, 15

Can you see where Carla's got it all wrong? She's blaming her lonely summers (and just about everything else) on something that cannot be changed. Carla would feel heaps better if she knew the following.

FACT 1: she doesn't have to hide away all summer, Carla chooses to hide away.

FACT 2: she doesn't have to wear trousers, she just has to be careful in the sun.

FACT 3: all that stuff about olive skin being really attractive is total nonsense!

Reinforcing the good

On a big piece of paper write down all your good points and don't let false modesty hold you back. Pin your list above the mirror in your room, read it and update it. It's not impossible to find something new and wonderful about yourself and your life every day.

Take a good look at your list and imagine that someone else had all these traits. Would you like them? Would you want to be friends with them? Of course you would!

CHAPTER SIX

Home and school

Some of us are blessed with teachers who encourage us to reach our potential, and parents who make sure that we believe in ourselves. Others are not so lucky.

They have teachers who yell and erode their confidence, and parents who put them down. In the end these kids believe that they have nothing to offer the world. They aren't even sure if the world has anything to offer them.

Whatever your situation, one thing is guaranteed: if you can improve your self-esteem on the school and home fronts, you'll

AAAAAAAGH!

be giving your future the biggest boost ever.

Greater self-esteem will give you:

- A firm belief in your own abilities.

- A feeling that you've got something to offer the world.

- A positive attitude that you can be and do whatever you work at.

- The strength to resist those who may try to control your life.

- An inner belief in yourself so the comments and opinions of others won't get you down.

- The courage to overcome a fear of failure.

School daze

"I can't wait to leave so that I can start living my life for real. No more parents and teachers telling me what to do!"
Paula, 14

 "I hate school even though I get high grades. The higher my marks, the more my friends hate me and call me a swot. They don't ask me to go out with them at the weekend and boys ignore me."
Lisa, 15

Do you hate school? If you do, it can help to work out just why it drives you mad. On the next couple of pages are three questions to which I've suggested some possible answers. See which ones best describe your feelings about school, teachers and the curriculum.

Question 1: What do you like about school?

Answer: "Nothing"

It's obvious that you're not getting the best (or anything) out of school, and maybe you're not putting enough into your school career either. Your teachers mightn't be giving you the attention you need, or you might be enrolled in the wrong subjects.

School is tough, horrible and boring, but – and, yes, you're going to hate me for saying this – it's there for your own good. School is life in miniature, and if you can work your way through its confusing corridors, make friends, get on with teachers and do your best in coursework and exams, then you're better equipped for life. No-one is saying that you have to be an 'A' student, only that you try your hardest.

If you're hiding your talents under a bushel as a way of hurting your parents or because you don't want your friends to think you're a swot, then you're only hurting yourself. You should work not to impress your teachers, parents or mates, but for yourself.

Answer: "Friends"

Sorry, you're on the wrong track. Social relationships are important, but so too are academic subjects.

Question 2: What's the high point of your school day?

Answer : "The going home bell"

Been there, said the same thing. I couldn't wait to escape, and if anyone had tried to convince me that school was full-to-bursting with high points I would have thought they were off their rocker (or paid to be there).

I found the lessons too hard, the teachers too boring and, above all, I didn't believe I was clever enough to pass the exams. For a while I stopped trying and got into trouble for skiving, not doing homework, flunking tests, causing trouble and talking too much in class.

Then I decided that if I really had to sit in a classroom until I was 18 years old, then I may as well pay a bit of attention. (Even day-dreaming becomes a chore after the first year or so.) What I discovered was hardly earth-shattering, but it was a revelation for me.

I discovered that I wasn't too bad at the subjects I hated (especially if I did the homework), and I was even pretty good at a few of them. The turning point came when I was 14 and had a poem printed in the school magazine. Suddenly I found that I had a talent. From then on, school made sense.

Answer: "P.E."

School doesn't have to be wonderful all the time. If you can find just one subject you like, and which you are willing to put some effort into, it can make a huge difference to your whole school career. It can make you realise that you have potential.

Question 3: Who is your favourite teacher and why?

Answer: "What planet did you say you're from?"

Even total pessimists can think of one teacher who inspired them or who they admire. For me, that teacher was Mr Phillips. Mr Phillips had no equal when it came to making it clear that everyone's opinion was valued. Until I joined his class I believed that teachers were always right (or thought they were) and that pupils were wrong. He also showed me that good teachers want to do more than just fill your head with facts. They want to be supportive, understanding and, above all, they want to encourage you to do your best. Giving them a chance to help is the first step in giving yourself a chance of success.

School stuff that can wear you down

"Boys are better than girls"

There is still a common misconception that boys do better than girls in education. If you ask a girl what she thinks, you can bet she will rate herself below her male classmates. But, national exam results don't reflect this at all. In fact, in some cases the opposite is true.

"I think boys do better at school because they are expected to. They don't mind being clever and they don't mind showing-off about it. I know that boys don't like clever girls. They hate girls who are smarter or funnier than them, so girls pretend they're not."
Allie, 16

"Boys are better at P.E., maths, science and art because they are sort of born knowing about this stuff. Girls are generally good at languages, but only because languages aren't nearly as difficult as physics and maths."
Sian, 15

Pressure to appear feminine, and myths about the difficulty of science and maths are just two of the many reasons we girls use to explain away poor academic performances. But to be fair we can't take all the blame. There are many people out there who are only too happy to confirm such myths.

If you believe what you hear, you automatically put a ceiling on your potential. Instead of saying, "I can do physics," you'll say: "Physics is a boy's subject so why should I waste my effort doing something that's too hard."

There are no subjects which are more suitable for one sex than the other. There are no hard and fast rules

about which sex does better at which subjects.
Success in a subject relies only on the following:

1. That you don't give up on a subject you find difficult.

2. That you ask for help when you need it.

3. That you understand you are not in competition with your classmates.

4. That you do your homework, participate in class discussions, and prepare for exams.

5. That you believe in your ability to do that subject, and ignore all advice to the contrary.

"I can't speak out in class"

"I hate getting things wrong in class. I feel really dumb and wish that the earth would open up and swallow me. Last year I made a big mistake in my history class and everyone laughed. I haven't spoken in class since."
Meera, 15

"I have a very quiet voice and when I go to answer a question, everyone asks me to speak up. It's almost a running gag. They may think it's funny, but I don't. On top of that, the boys shout me down before I can finish saying my piece."
Paula, 14

Being embarrassed and afraid of failing holds people

back from contributing in class. However, not speaking out has far-reaching effects outside the classroom. It can stop you standing up for yourself and your beliefs, and it can make you miss opportunities. If you let the fear of failure (the fear of getting something wrong or saying something embarrassing) overwhelm you at school, it will overwhelm you in everything you do.

The things to remember are:

- It is not the end of the world if you give an incorrect answer.

- Not understanding something isn't a sign of stupidity. Not asking for help is stupid.

- Embarrassment is only momentary.

- No-one remembers the things you get wrong.

- Speaking in front of people gets easier the more you do it.

- If someone shouts you down, assert yourself and ask them to let you finish.

Teachers

"Our teachers tell us we're all the same, but they don't really mean it. For a start, they treat boys differently, letting them shout and make a racket. On the other hand, teachers tell off

the girls for chatting. I complained to one teacher and she said,
'Well, boys are just more disruptive than girls', as if that were
an excuse."
Sharon, 16

"When I told my careers' teacher that I wanted to be an
actress, he laughed and said it was a silly idea. Not only was I
too shy apparently, but I wasn't very good at English and I
didn't live in London. He went on to say that I'd be better off
being a teacher or a social worker. I was so depressed."
Lisa, 16

Teachers – love them or loathe them – affect your life
in a big way. Good teachers are worth their weight in
gold. Bad teachers are cheating you not only of a
good education, but also ruining your chances of a
good career. If you've got a bad teacher, tell your
parents and arrange to get together with your form
tutor or school counsellor.

This is what you have to know about teachers:

• Teachers don't know everything about everything.
  They certainly might not be well-informed about
  non-academic career opportunities like acting.

• Ignore teachers who put you down for poor
  performance in their subject. As long as you believe
  you're doing your best that's all that counts. It's
  also worth remembering that you're bound to be
  better at some subjects than others. I was lousy at
  maths (still am), but eventually aced it in science

and English. My best friend could put Michelangelo to shame in the art room, but had to work long and hard to come to grips with geography. (Like I said, she was a genius with a paint brush, but she had trouble finding the art block.)

- Just because your teachers don't believe in you, it doesn't mean that you're going to fail your exams. I know plenty of people who were told they would never amount to much only to have gone on to fulfil their dreams in a certain career or at a college or university.

- Teachers are human; they have good days and they have bad days. That's just the way it is.

Bullying and sexual harassment

"I have been bullied since my first day at senior school. The girls pick on me for no reason, and I don't know what to do. I feel useless and ashamed."
Helen, 15

Bullying and sexual harassment totally destroy self-confidence and self-esteem, and have lasting effects on the victim. If you are being bullied then you need to tell an adult (parents or teachers) immediately. Don't let the bullies get you down – take on board this five-point plan:

- You are not to blame for what's happening. You are innocent.

- Bullies thrive and rely on their victims' silence. Deny them that satisfaction and speak out to a trusted adult.

- There is no rhyme or reason as to why you have been chosen by the bullies. Sometimes it has to do with your nationality, your skin colour or your beliefs, but often there is no specific cause. Don't start to question yourself or to believe what they say.

- Don't give bullies the opportunity to get at you. Stay in the company of your friends, don't run away, and don't even think about threatening bullies in return.

- If your complaints of bullying or sexual harassment are falling on deaf ears, don't give up. Keep telling your story until someone takes action.

To swot or not!

"I'm really clever but I've never been out with a boy. My friends say it's because I am too smart and boys don't like

egg-heads. I agree, but don't know what to do about it.
If I flunk out my parents will go mad, but not having a
date is driving me mad."
Sharma, 16

"I'm unbelievably stupid. No wonder the kids in my class call
me 'Thicko'. I can't find even one subject that I'm good at. I
think it would be best if I just left school."
Hannah, 15

Sometimes it doesn't matter what you do, you just
can't win. If you're too clever there are drawbacks. If
you're 'dumb' life's no bowl of cherries either. But if
you think that giving yourself an I.Q. make-over is
going to make your friends love you and cause boys
to fall at your feet, you're wrong. Lying to others
means lying to yourself, and that really dents your
sense of self-esteem.

If friends of either sex don't like you for who you are,
they don't deserve you.

Forget the make-over, remember these instead:

- The words 'swot' or 'thicko' are just like other terms
  of abuse – they are not worth getting hung up about.

- Schools, teachers, parents and society in general
  place an awful lot of emphasis on school as being a
  make-or-break situation. It's just not true. Not
  everyone finds their career goal or develops to their
  full potential while at school.

- Even though schools are geared toward academic work and higher education, it doesn't mean that it isn't able to help you pursue non-academic subjects. For example, look at the new stuff you can do in Pre-Vocational Studies.

Physical education

"We have P.E. three times a week and each time it's a nightmare. I'm rubbish when it comes to anything sporty. I can't run, I can't catch a ball and no-one ever picks me for their team. When I do get a chance to play, I can hear everyone moaning on the sidelines. If the team loses, I get the blame. P.E. is making me a nervous wreck."
Sue, 16

Sport causes more bad memories, especially among girls, than all other school subjects combined. Oddly, it is also the subject where low self-esteem is at an all-time high.

At a period in your development when exercise has been proved to be extremely beneficial to your health (and to your self-esteem), it's sad to think that so many girls are being put off.

Why do you hate P.E. and expend so much effort trying to worm out of it? Is it because your teacher or class mates humiliate you? Is it because you think all the others are sporting naturals? Is it because you hate all that communal undressing and showering? Once you know the exact reason for your P.E. phobia you can start doing something about it. Here are a few ideas to get you started:

- Not all gym teachers are heartless bullies, but if one is giving you undue grief you can do something about it. You have rights and can report them to your year head or tell your parents.

- Physical exercise can improve how you feel about yourself. Try for just one lesson to put all your fears behind you. Imagine you are a P.E. superhero. A change of attitude could change your game.

- Team games like netball, football and hockey teach you how to work with other people. Sometimes it's plain sailing, at other times it's one big Rugby scrum where everyone's fighting for the ball.

- Heckling from the sidelines is uncalled for, and any half-decent teacher will put a stop to it immediately. Likewise any attempts to exclude certain players from the team.

- Everyone performs differently on the field and in the changing room. Some seem totally relaxed with the undressing routine, others struggle to undress without revealing so much as a naked ankle. The only way to go is the way that makes you feel comfortable.

Family matters

Schools, mates and boyfriends are small fry when it comes to killing your esteem. The real sharks are your family: doting fathers who are over-protective, well-intentioned mums who go overboard on criticism, and sisters and brothers who tease you mercilessly or are held up as exemplary role models.

To see how your family fares on the esteem-front, grab a pen and paper and do this quiz. If you feel in the mood for grilling your family, hit them with question 8.

1. You're at the cinema with all your mates when you suddenly catch sight of your parents. What do you do?

a) Hide in your popcorn before they get a chance to embarrass you.

b) Go over and say hello.

c) Ignore them.

2. Which best describes your relationship with your family?

a) Mostly happy, though sometimes they can be unbelievably annoying.

b) The pits – lots of arguments followed by long silences.

c) Sort of ordinary and boring.

3. You buy a new dress that's short and tight. What do your parents say?

a) "You're not going out like that!"

b) Nothing. They wouldn't notice.

c) Comment that your legs are not thin enough for such a short skirt.

4. What would really freak your parents out?

a) You fail an exam or get a detention.

b) You have your belly-button pierced and dye your hair acid blue.

c) Nothing much – they don't care what you do.

5. When you fail an exam, how do your parents react?

a) They don't react – they over-react!

b) They want to know what went wrong, and if there is anything they can do to help.

c) They wouldn't – you won't have told them.

6. If you could change one thing about your parents what would it be?

a) You'd choose not to have any.

b) You'd make them calmer and less stressed out.

c) You're not sure.

7. Do you think your parents know the real you?

a) Pretty much.

b) No.

c) You bet!

8. How many of the following can your parents correctly name or answer?

- Your best friend.
- Your worst enemy.
- Your worst habit.
- What you want to be.
- How old you are next birthday.
- The name of the boy you fancy.
- Your favourite pop star.
- Your weakest point.
- Your best subject.
- What after-school clubs you belong to.

How many did they get right?
a)   Nine or more.
b)   Three or less.
c)   Between four and eight.

SCORES

1.	a 10	b 5	c 0
2.	a 5	b 0	c 10
3.	a 10	b 0	c 5
4.	a 10	b 5	c 0
5.	a 10	b 5	c 0
6.	a 0	b 10	c 5
7.	a 5	b 0	c 10
8.	a 10	b 0	c 5

What your score means

0-20

Your parents could be seriously zapping your self-esteem by ignoring your needs. You need to wake them up (and you'd better be quick about it) to the fact that you need their support and encouragement. It might help if you talk to them, instead of ignoring them.

25-60

You seem to have a good honest and balanced relationship with your family. Not too distant, but not too in-your-face. Keep up the good work.

65-80

Your parents may be a little too involved in your life. Their desire to be close may be smothering you. Try to put a little distance between yourself and them by not sharing all your deepest thoughts.

Handling your family

"There are times when my dad just drives me crazy. He's always telling me to be careful. And every time I start something new, he tells me what to do and what not to do. He doesn't trust me to look after myself."
Donna, 17

What do you do when your parents (or sisters and brothers) go heavy on the criticism and crush your new-found confidence? Do you storm around, slam doors, burst into tears, and go totally ballistic? Well, if you do you're on a hiding to nothing. Try one of these well-tested family handling strategies instead.

Have a little empathy

Parents sometimes react or behave according to something that is going on in their own lives. (Yes, parents do have a life!) So extend a little sympathy and empathy, and try to worm out of them the reason for their totally blinkered and off-the-wall behaviour.

Flash your birth certificate

Remind them you are growing up and are developing your own ideas about who you want to be and what you're going to wear. Loving parents hold on to their memories of you as a cuddly little baby so tightly that they forget that you're an independent person who can think for herself.

Give them a sensible piece of your mind

If your mum or dad goes on at you about your weight, looks or school work, talk to them calmly and sensibly. Tell them that their remarks really upset you, and point out that their constant criticism is wearing down your self-esteem.

Strut your stuff responsibly

If your parents are over-protective and refuse to let you out of their sight, then a bit of careful negotiation by example is in order. Show them you are responsible and mature by telling them where you're going, leaving contact numbers, sticking to curfews and not doing anything reckless.

You're beyond comparison

If you are being compared to an older sister or brother it can be soul destroying. But don't fall into the all-too-common trap of trying to imitate them. It won't work. You are a unique individual with your own strengths and talents. Copying a sibling to get into your parents' good books will only annoy your role model and cause even more trouble. Respect yourself for what you are and let your parents know that you are proud of your achievements. Give credit where credit's due by congratulating siblings on their successes.

It ain't no joke!

Teasing has the same effect as constant bullying. If you feel a parent or a sibling is picking on you, then talk to them. Explain that you don't find their jibes amusing, and ask them to stop. All too often teasers carry on simply because they think you're in on the joke.

Being different is good

If you feel so embarrassed about your background that it's sapping your confidence, then it's time to do some serious thinking. What is it that's making you cringe? Are your parents too old, too poor, too rich? Do they speak with an accent? Hard as it may be, try not to be ashamed of them because this will only lead you to feel ashamed of yourself. Accept your family for what they are, and look at their uniqueness as a positive not a negative thing. No-one's parents are the same, just as no two people are the same. Be proud of who they are, and in turn be proud of yourself. It also helps to remember that you do things which must make your parents want to hide under a rock.

They expect too much!

Parents want their kids to do well, but in order to make their kids high achievers they pile on the pressure. Too much pressure leads to their children feeling inadequate and totally lacking in self-confidence.

> "My parents are desperate for me to be a doctor, but they don't seem to understand that I'm not smart enough to get the necessary grades. I want to tell them, but I'm scared that they'll be really disappointed. To protect them I pretend that I'm doing better than I am."
> Claire, 16

Parental expectations have a lot to do with your parents' dreams. They dream that you will have a better life than they have had. They dream you will do something that they weren't able to do. They dream of you making their dreams come true. All this is totally unfair, but all parents (yes, even the level-headed ones) plan out their children's future. Problem is, they do it without your consent.

If your parents are giving you a hard time, find out why. Then tell them you're doing your best, and that you'd really like to make up your own mind about what the future holds for you. It's going to be hard (and take some courage) to stand up for yourself like this, but it's even harder to live up to someone else's expectations.

A plan for family harmony

1. Talk to them.

2. Give them a break. Everyone has a bad day, and they may just be taking it out on you.

3. Learn to see yourself as an individual as well as a member of the family unit. Once you do, it will be easier to accept your family, warts and all.

4. Stand up for yourself and what you believe in. At the same time, respect the opinions of others.

5. Be honest about what you want and why.

6. Don't take out your bad moods on your family.

7. Parents and older siblings don't know everything.

8. Love them or loathe them, they're your family for life.

Your future

You're now pretty knowledgeable about upping your self-esteem in any situation, so what's next? Well, how about your future? Want to make all your dreams come true (or at least make a start on them)?

Choosing a career is tough, especially when you're not sure where your talents lie. To find your talents and interests, and to get your future on the agenda, you have to focus, plan, take action and, most importantly, learn to work around set-backs.

Focus

If you think you're a no-talent human, think again. Everyone in this world has talents. Some are great with numbers, others are brilliant with words, yet more have the gift of the gab. Like I said, think again but this time don't be so hard on yourself.

On a piece of paper write down all the things you think you're good at, and all the things that others have complimented you on. This is not the time for false modesty – strut your stuff proudly. For example, "I'm a good shopper, a great listener, and very musical. My teacher says I write wonderful poems."

Now write a list of the things you loved doing when you were younger, or things you love doing now. For example, "I love reading, travelling and designing clothes."

By looking at both lists you will get a good indication of the areas in which you might like to work. For instance, if you like reading, ask yourself what it is about reading that makes it so enjoyable. Is it the joy of being taken into imaginary worlds, or the information that can be absorbed? If it's one of these your future might lie in writing, teaching or researching. If you like reading because you like books, maybe you'd be happy as a librarian or as a book editor.

Plan

It's no good hoping that someone will walk through your bedroom door and offer you your career on a plate. No, you've got to plan, be organised and informed.

1. Read up on the job you want.

2. Write to companies you'd like to work for, asking for information about necessary qualifications and skills. If you want a reply, include a stamped self-addressed envelope.

3. If you know someone who is already employed in your dream job, ask them for all the inside information.

4. Make sure you take subjects that will let you pursue your career dream.

Take action

Planning without action goes nowhere. Planning with action goes everywhere. Taking action does not mean you have to take quantum leaps to get huge returns. All that's needed are lots of small steps in the right direction. Not only are they easier to achieve (large goals sometimes seem so far out of your grasp that you give up), but you can make changes in direction as you go.

For instance, if you are worried about rainforests and want to save them, the task may seem so daunting that it's impossible. On the other hand, you can start small by doing something for your local environment, like starting a recycling group or volunteering for a local environment charity. The inevitable success of your first eco-warrior venture will give you the confidence, the know-how and the contacts to act on behalf of bigger projects farther afield.

Let's say you wanted to be an actor, you could join the school drama group. One season treading the boards (may as well use the lingo of the business) in the school hall will give you the necessary experience to join a local dramatic society. It may not be the West End or Broadway or Hollywood, but every little bit helps spur you onward and upward.

... and I'd like to thank....

DRAMA CLUB
4.30 FRIDAY
ROOM 2B
(OR NOT 2B, THAT IS THE QUESTION).

Working around setbacks

Very few people reach the pinnacle of their career without having tried and failed a couple of times. We've all heard stories about the Booker prize-winning author whose first ten manuscripts were rejected, and about the athletes who lose races and sponsorship deals time and again before finally hitting a winning streak.

Disappointments are something we all have to deal with, but a disappointment only becomes a failure if you let it. If you didn't get an interview for a particular college and then made no attempt to find an alternative, then you've failed. But if you bundled up your disappointment and tossed it into the nearest skip, learnt a lesson or two, and then went out to find another way to fulfil your dream, that's not failure. That's working around setbacks.

Another lesson to learn is that it is wrong to blame yourself for everything bad that happens ("It's all my fault. I'm just not good enough. Sob, sob."). Sometimes the reason lies elsewhere.

For example, not everyone can come first, gain entry to particular colleges, win prizes, and impress theatre directors at auditions. If you have chosen to work in a creative industry, then coping with rejection notes is part of the job specification. It's not that you weren't 'good enough', but that perhaps your style of writing or acting was not suitable on that occasion. You haven't failed, it's just that your time has yet to come. In the vocational careers, like medicine, law and teaching, there are strict standards that have to be kept. This means that some will make it, others won't. As the saying goes, "If at first you don't succeed, try, try, and try again." I saw another version of this the other day and it went like this: "If at first you don't succeed, you're running at about average."

If you let a setback turn into a failure, you only have yourself to blame. It's heart-breaking and humiliating when things go wrong, but it's a part of life. If you can learn to cope (and smile), you can cope with anything.

CHAPTER SEVEN

Positive thinking

This chapter is all about giving you the motivation to keep your self-esteem on a happy high every day. It's all very well knowing how to cope in extraordinary situations, but how do you stay on top of the day-in, day-out hassles that wear you down bit by bit? For instance, how do you handle yourself at the hairdressers or in other places where it pays to be self-assured and politely assertive? And how about those times when you're home alone on a Saturday night; how do you stop yourself from falling into despair and watching repeats of the snooker?

Not only will the following information help you to stay positive, it will also help you

HEY, IT'S SATURDAY NIGHT. HAVEN'T YOU GOT ANY FRIENDS TO GO OUT WITH?

VCR

to like yourself a whole lot more. You'll be so chuffed with yourself and so relaxed in your own company that you won't mind one bit when you have some time to yourself on a Saturday night!

Six things you have to remember:

1. Be a positive person, not a pessimist.
2. Don't be hard on yourself when someone upsets you.
3. Being bitchy and critical about others says more about you than about them.
4. Don't revel in guilt or self-pity.
5. Be assertive, not aggressive.
6. Being alone does not mean you're some sort of social outcast doomed to a life of abject misery.

You are what you say

Being positive is not just looking in the mirror and saying to yourself "I'm great." It's also how you speak about yourself, how you influence others through what you say, and how you raise or lower your self-esteem by the things you say.

Most people underestimate the impact of their speech. Words and language, however, are extremely meaningful because for most of us they are our main tools of communication. You can change your mood and the way others see you by simply saying "I'm depressed".

If you use a certain phrase or word over and over (for example, "I'm stupid" or "I'm bored") you will begin to feel like that. In short: you are what you say.

Listen to yourself and spot those phrases which seem to roll off your tongue automatically. You know the kind – the ones you use repeatedly when someone asks how you are, or what you're doing, or what's new. Once you become conscious of them you will see that many are unjustified. Draw up a list of these phrases and ask yourself whether you really meant what you said. Did you really do 'nothing' at the weekend? Were you really bored in English on Thursday? Okay, so English on Thursday might not have been wildly scintillating, but was it really boring? Chances are you used the word 'boring' out of sheer habit.

A good word in your ear

If you say mean things about yourself you are, in effect, hurting yourself more than you know. Think of all the negative ways you describe yourself to others, and write them down. A 16-year-old friend of mine came up with these words to describe herself: difficult, nosy, nervy, and miserable. If there are nasty negative words on your list, replace them with more positive words. For example, instead of 'difficult' use 'challenging': same meaning, but more positive. Have a look at the following list to get the idea.

Negative word	Positive equivalent
Chatter-box	Good communicator
Difficult	Challenging

Nosy	Curious
Nervy	Full of energy
Miserable	Upset
"This is boring!"	"I've got to make this interesting"!
"I hate..."	"I don't like..."
"It annoys me when you..."	"I'd prefer it if you..."

Using positive language is the first step toward positive thinking. In essence, positive thinking is seeing dark thunderous clouds, but thinking "Oh good, this will help break the drought," rather than "Oh, no I hate the rain." It's about looking on the bright side and of being full of hope.

Positive thinking also means not letting the actions or reactions of others get you down. The world is full of miserable souls who delight in making those around them equally miserable. No matter what the situation they will see the sad, bad and mean side of it. Worse still they'll do it in order to protect themselves.

For example, Miss Negative may say, "Oh, you don't want to do that. It's too hard. You'll stuff up and make an idiot of yourself." What she's really saying is: "I'm too afraid to do it, so I'm not going to let you do it in case you succeed and show me up."

In order to be a positive thinker you have to make yourself see the upside of a situation. However, this doesn't mean ignoring the bad and pretending it doesn't exist. A positive thinker will imagine themselves doing well in an exam, but should they do badly in a mock they won't pretend that they didn't get a poor mark. Instead, they will take notice of what they did wrong, correct it and know that they will do better in the final exam.

"I used to be a huge worrier – everything was a drama. I would worry about stupid things like being late, not wearing the right clothes or being cold-shouldered by my mates. Then my mum had a long talk with me. She said, 'What's the point in worrying about the future. If the worst happens then you'll have worried twice. If the best happens, you'll have worried for nothing.' Mum was right. Worrying is a waste of time."
Paula, 17

Don't be hard on yourself

"Every time I do something wrong I get so mad with myself. I think, 'Idiot, idiot, idiot - why on earth did you do that?' My friends tell me I have to give myself a break, but I don't know how."
Nicola, 15

Most of us are our own worst enemy. We don't give ourselves a break, we can't forgive our mistakes and worse still, we don't allow ourselves to fail.

Are you someone who:
- Never acknowledges their talents?
- Makes a big to-do about their mistakes?

- Can't take a compliment?
- Always thinks everyone else is better?
- Hides (or thinks they're hiding) their real personality and thoughts?
- Worries that they're going to be exposed as a fraud?

If you answered 'yes' to any of the above, you're knocking yourself for no reason. You've failed to understand that we learn from our mistakes and grow through our failures. Stuffing up a relationship, an exam or your Saturday job does not mean you are useless and therefore deserve less out of life.

Disappointments are hard to forget, and achievements are often overlooked. Humans find it easier and more comfortable to be mean to themselves than to be nice. This is partly because most of us are brought up to believe that good people are modest people, and modest people conceal their achievements. This makes us push our successes so far aside that we forget we have them. The way to combat this is simple: keep a check-list of all the wonderful things you do each day.

Don't simply jot down that at last you've understood logic gates. Your list should cover everything that made you smile, gave you a warm feeling or made you proud. Did you, for example, not lay into your younger sister for using your brush? Did you forgive someone for gossiping behind your back? Or better still, did you forgive yourself for mucking up the last answer on the test?

Refer to this check-list whenever you start being hard on yourself. The moment Miss Negative rears her head, grab your list and read the biography of an outstandingly wonderful person – you!

Critic, heal thyself

When you criticise others you're showing your own insecurities. By pointing the finger at someone else (especially those who have similar flaws to your own), you're diverting attention away from yourself. If you are always noticing everyone's faults, you're probably not too proud of yourself.

If you can accept your own weaknesses, you're less likely to be bothered by those of others. To zero in on your ever-so-minor imperfections, ask yourself the following questions. Once again you'll need a pen and paper.

1: Think of the person who irritates you the most.
2: What do they do that drives you mad?
3: Why should they change this annoying behaviour?
4: Does their behaviour remind you of yourself?

When we say or think mean things about others it makes us feel guilty and causes our insecurities to grow. As a result, we become harder on ourselves. The next step (down!) is to be even nastier about others and, in turn, even meaner to ourselves.

Our criticisms of ourselves and of others is linked to our expectations. If we choose to force our expectations or opinions on to others, we will always be disappointed because people will fail to live up to them. This is what happened to Maria (15) and her best friend Donna.

> *"I thought Donna and I would always be best mates. I told her everything, and I thought she was as open with me. Then a few weeks ago I found out that she got a boyfriend over the summer holidays. Donna hadn't even mentioned it."*

Maria is not angry with her friend for having a boyfriend, but angry because Donna didn't live up to her expectations. Maria felt that she had been honest with Donna, but is hurt that Donna didn't return the trust. What happened here is that the two girls had different opinions about what being best friends means. Maria assumed that friends had no secrets; Donna thought something different. No one's at fault, they just had different expectations.

To get your mind working on this terribly knotty problem of expectations, think about the following questions.

Do people have the right to believe in anything they want, and to behave in any way they want?

How many friends have you written off or criticised because they behaved differently from what you expected?

Is it right that you should demand certain things from certain people? For example, honesty from your friends, love from your parents, or faithfulness from your boyfriend?

Be assertive, not aggressive

Assertiveness is the skill of being able to politely insist that your opinions be valued and responded to. Thankfully, it is a skill which can be learnt. And once learnt it will give you a chance of getting what you want. It will also put a stop to people using you as a doormat and wiping their feet on your self-esteem.

When you're being assertive you use lots of communication skills (for example, body language), but you do not use aggression, disrespect, rudeness, bossiness or stroppiness. Nor do you make your point by shouting.

Be assertive...

...not aggressive

Assertive people are :	Aggressive people are:
Calmly spoken	Angry and loud
Open	Manipulative
Polite	Rude
Firm	Stubborn
Co-operative	Bullying
Respectful of others	Disrespectful and intolerant
Good listeners	Too busy ranting to listen

So before you lose your cool in a testing situation, take some time out to plan an assertive – not aggressive – strategy.

ASSERTIVENESS STEP 1: Decide what the issue is. For example, "I want my friend to know that she can't walk all over me any more."

ASSERTIVENESS STEP 2: Decide if your complaint is fair. Look carefully at the whole issue to make sure that you've played no part in causing the friction.

ASSERTIVENESS STEP 3: Decide if assertive behaviour is appropriate with this particular person.

If your hassles involve a bully, then any sort of direct approach is likely to end with you being further bullied, or even hurt. In this instance you really must seek help from an adult. And I don't mean an adult who will be aggressive on your behalf.

ASSERTIVENESS STEP 4: What do you want to happen as a result of your assertive behaviour?

For example, "After I speak to my friend I want her to understand how I feel (upset and hurt) and for her to stop using me. I also want her to know that I still want to be friends." You could, of course, want her to understand your feelings but still want out of the friendship. It's important that you're clear about what you want. If you're not, you won't be able to present your gripe firmly, clearly and with conviction.

ASSERTIVENESS STEP 5: Work out exactly what you're going to say. Put yourself in the other person's shoes, imagine what their reactions will be and try to plan your responses in advance.

ASSERTIVENESS STEP 6: Don't be rude or turn into a bully. Stay calm. Be ready to give constructive criticism, but also be prepared to tolerate a bit of destructive criticism.

Assertive communication includes the magic of body language. If you want to make the best possible impression, the only way to do it is to look people in the eye, to stand tall and to keep still. No one's going to trust a person who avoids eye contact, slouches, shuffles and fidgets.

Assertiveness is an important aspect of your self-respect because it's about confirming your rights. Everyone has rights, and though priorities may be different there are many 'expectations' that we all hold in common. Some of these are included in the following list. Go through the 'Bill of Rights', tick those that are important to you, and add any ideas of your own. When your list is complete, design a 'Bill of Rights' poster and put it somewhere prominent.

My Bill of Rights

I have a right to be treated well.
I have a right to be listened to.
I have a right to ask for something,

even though I might not get it.
I have a right to privacy.
I have a right to make up my own mind.
I have a right to be happy.
I have a right to be different.

The 'Bill of Rights' is a guide map for your life. It should contain all the positive things you believe in and want to work towards. When you feel down, chances are that one of your rights has been abused. For instance, if you've written "I have the right to my own opinion," you'll know exactly why you feel annoyed when someone tells you you're wrong.

The final item on your 'Bill of Rights' should be: "In return for these rights, I will respect the rights of others."

Difficult feelings

"I get so angry all the time. My mum says I've got a problem and that I have to learn to calm down. But no matter how hard I try, something happens and I explode."
Cara, 17

Anger is one of the primary emotions and despite its reputation it isn't a bad emotion. Like joy, pain and happiness, anger is a natural response to certain events. And just as expressing your happiness makes you feel good, it's better to express your anger rather than bottle it up where it ferments into nastiness.

Okay, so we all agree that it's good to express your anger, the trouble comes when you act on your anger by taking it out on others or yourself. People who say "I couldn't help it, I was angry" made a choice to act out their anger. If this sounds like you, then it may help to look at exactly why you lash out and what you hope to achieve when you do. Rather than hit out or have a door-slamming session (which, in the end, only leads to further trouble and greater loss of self-respect), walk away, count to ten, have a quiet think, and work out an assertive plan of action.

Frustration

"Sometimes I feel so frustrated I could scream. I feel like I'm trapped and that no-one can hear what I'm saying."
Lena, 16

Feeling frustrated comes from being misunderstood, ignored, or from being unable to achieve desired goals. Often a sense of frustration comes about because we don't really know what our goals are, so we thrash about trying different things only to find that we're still not satisfied.

To give frustration its marching orders you have to accept that long-term happiness and fulfilment come from within, and not from boyfriends, new clothes, make-up, careers, money or from going out. If you work at getting to know yourself (and liking what you find), then you won't look elsewhere for happiness.

Disappointment

> "I'm always disappointed. Friends let me down, and situations don't go as planned. I was really looking forward to going to a new school, but now that I'm there it's no big deal."
> Liz, 15

If you depend on people or events to improve or dramatically change your situation or feelings, then disappointment will follow disappointment. You're investing too much in others. What you have to do is take responsibility for your life – the good times and the bad – and learn to accept that you alone can change your life.

If you don't set your friends on towering pedestals, then they won't let you down. If you don't hang your whole social life on just one hot date, then you won't be disappointed. If you accept yourself (and that means accepting that you might have a little bit of work to do on changing your negative attitude or upping your self-esteem), then you'll never be disappointed.

Possessiveness

> "I am so possessive of my things, my friends and my family. It's because of my insane jealousy that I've lost so many boyfriends. I hate myself for being this way. What can I do?"
> Sharon, 15

Possessiveness and fear go hand-in-hand. When we are possessive about a certain person and don't want to share them with others, it's because we are afraid of losing them to someone 'better'. If there was ever a time for boosting self-esteem, this is it.

Not only is the person talking and thinking themselves down, they are totally underestimating their friend. The sort of conversation the possessive person has with themselves goes like this: "I'm nothing special and have very little going for me, therefore anyone I manage to befriend is going to be pretty low themselves. So low, in fact, that they'll dump me when they find someone better." Are we talking desperate here, or are we talking desperate?

FACT 1: Love isn't about owning someone.

FACT 2: If you love someone and they love you, there's no need to feel insecure.

FACT 3: If you are clinging onto someone because you're afraid of being alone, then you don't love yourself enough.

FACT 4: Possessiveness and self-esteem are polar opposites. Once you have self-esteem you won't need to be possessive. If you believe that you're a worthwhile and lovable person of the first order you don't have to rely on other people to prove it.

CHAPTER EIGHT

Making progress

People who don't know anything about self-esteem often sneer at books like this one. They wrongly believe that improving your self-esteem means being selfish. Nothing, of course, could be further from the truth.

Sure, self-esteem and self-respect are primarily about you, but as none of us is an island they are also about everyone else. For example, our behaviour, attitude and communication skills have a ripple effect and if you send out good vibes others will feel them and benefit. If you're mean to someone, they will feel bad and in turn go on to be mean to someone else.

This is why self-esteem is so important. If you like yourself, you will like others. If you respect yourself, you will respect others. If you accept nothing is perfect, you won't look for perfection in others. To make the world a better place, you have to start with yourself and work outwards.

High self-esteem:

- Makes you a more generous person.
- Makes you kinder to others.
- Gives you energy.
- Makes you positive.
- Helps you to be honest and open with people, and vice versa.

Take risks – Who dares wins

How courageous are you? Are you known as some-one who has a dare-devil spirit? Someone who takes risks? If you have low self-esteem, the chances are that you're not a risk-taker but would like to be.

People who take risks (not reckless risks, mind you) aren't afraid of failing. They may not get on the swimming squad, but they know that such a setback isn't going to dint their self-esteem (remember, self-esteem is not dependent on outside successes), or make them hide away in total embarrassment. Their self-esteem will help them to get over the bad try-out and set them up for other challenges.

If you don't take risks, you'll never know what you're capable of doing. If you don't audition for the drama society, you'll never know if you've got the makings of a great actress. Win or lose, risk-takers always win because each challenge makes them a stronger person. Courage isn't about being fearless, it's about doing something even if you're scared to death.

If you would like to be a risk-taker, try this exercise.

Write down something you would love to do if you weren't scared. For example, act in the school play, speak out in class, or ask out someone you like.

Write down what's the worst that could happen if you did take a risk. For example, are you worried that your mates will laugh at your audition, or that your possible date will reject you? Do you think that one failure will mean failure in everything? (If you do, then go back and re-read this book!)

Now work out the best and happiest ending for your story. For example, for your performance in the play you receive a standing ovation; for answering a question in class you get lots of encouragement from your teacher and classmates; and when you ask the love of your life out on a date, he jumps at the chance of spending some quality one-to-one time with you.

What you've got to do now is weigh up the pros (the positive outcomes) against the cons (the negative outcomes) by giving each a mark out of ten. The one with the highest score, wins.

Let's say that the fear of having your mates laugh at your audition isn't really all that scary and you give it a score of two out of ten. (After all what's a bit of harmless chuckling between friends?) On the other hand, receiving a standing ovation is worth nine out of ten. Obviously then, trying out for the school play is worth the risk because you've got heaps to gain (nine), and little to lose (two).

If any of your positive outcomes scores four or less, don't attempt it yet. You're most probably not really ready to accept all eventualities, and possibly not totally committed to it anyway. Try something else.

Stand up for yourself

Are you someone who can't do enough for other people? Do you always put the needs of others first? Are you the classroom agony aunt who listens to everyone's gripes? Do you feel that no-one is ever there when you need a shoulder to cry on?

If any of these ring a bell, it's time for you to look at why you spend so much energy helping others.

First, if you do it in order to feel good, then you've got to make some changes. You've got to stop investing your happiness and fulfilment in others. You have to take charge yourself.

Second, all this activity makes it impossible for you to look at the state of your life. When you're so involved with the problems of others, you don't have to face your own. As we mentioned in chapter two, being constantly on-the-go means that you don't have the time to think about yourself.

Third, putting the needs of others before your own and not standing up for your rights is an announcement to the world that you don't think very highly of your own problems, opinions, feelings, and ultimately yourself.

And finally, a person who is always helping often does it because they need to feel needed. When they don't get the appreciative feedback that they so desperately require, they are resentful and hurt.

When you help someone for the right reasons, there is no expectation of reward or self-interested satisfaction, only the pleasure of having helped.

All this boils down to the difference between being a genuinely caring person and one who simply appears to be well-meaning. Have a look at the following list to see the difference.

The pretender	A genuine person
Pretends to agree when they don't.	Is honest.
Says 'yes' to everything.	Is selective.
Lets people take advantage of them.	Asserts their rights.
Talks about their good deeds.	Says nothing.
Lives through others.	Lives their own life.

Once you learn to look after yourself, you'll know how to look after others.

Want, want, want — who needs it?

Learning to tell the difference between a need and a want puts you on the right road to being happy with who you are. Our lives are full of things we think we just have to have. The simple truth is that most of our desires are totally unnecessary to our well-being.

Grab a pen and paper and write down your current needs/wants. Your list might include boyfriend, designer label clothing, a more shapely figure, money, brains, friends.

Take a hard look at each item and ask yourself the following questions:

How vital is it to my existence?

Will I die without it?

If I were given this item right now, would it solve all my problems?

Why do I need it so badly? (If it's to raise your self-esteem by making people like you more, then what you've got is low, low self-esteem. Admit it.)

Many things we think we need are just wants – things that we feel would make our lives better and happier. What we do is convince ourselves that we can't be happy without 'x'. But do you really need 'x' to continue living? Not likely unless you're talking about food, water and protection. A need is a matter of survival, a want is simply an unnecessary desire.

If you can distinguish needs from wants, then you'll be able to live in the present. After all, what's the point in wishing for the future when you have to live right now?

Home alone – it's really okay

If you're in tune with half the world's population your biggest anxiety will have something to do with being lonely, dateless, and on your own.

Most of us grow up with the notion that it's not right to be on your own. That it's not okay to stay in on a Saturday night and to spend your free time in your own company. As a result, we fill our lives with activities and acquaintances that are often as exciting as watching paint dry.

To be alone, we think, is to be a failure. Better, we say to ourselves, to pretend to like someone or something than to admit to having nothing to do or no-one to be with.

This attitude is wrong, wrong, wrong.

To like your own company and to be happy spending time on your own are both signs that you like and respect yourself. I know it won't go down well when you tell your supposed friends that you'd prefer to read a good book than watch a film on T.V. with them, but go on, try it. What's the worst that can happen? Your friends will get square eyes and their brains will shrivel up like walnuts, while you spend an afternoon with your feet up reading a great book and plucking your eyebrows (not at the same time, of course).

Here are the simple and straightforward facts about spending some time in your own company:

1. Spending some time on your own doesn't mean doing nothing at all (unless of course, doing nothing is what you want to do). It means having the time to do everything you want to do.

2. The first step in being comfortable on your own is to stop driving yourself crazy wondering what everyone else is up to and what you're missing.

3. Being alone and being lonely are two different things. Being alone is a state of being; loneliness is a feeling that can occur whether you're by yourself or with a crowd of friends. A sense of loneliness comes from being misunderstood or feeling that you're somehow different.

If you feel lonely all the time, is it because you keep your darkest fears to yourself? If this sounds like you, then you must open up to someone.

4. If you can't bear to spend any time on your own – and it is important that you do – start out by promising yourself just 30 minutes of time alone a day. This will help you to get into the habit of being on your own. It's a bit like getting to know a new friend. You don't rush in and spend 24 hours a day, seven days a week with them. You first meet for a couple of hours once a week and take it from there.

Give yourself a pat on the back

A good way to reinforce positive feelings about yourself is to value all your skills. Just because you're naturally good at something you devalue it by saying, "Oh, anyone could do that." The fact is, not just anyone did it, YOU did, so take a bow and accept the accolades.

To remind yourself of all the things you can do, make a list and hang it somewhere you can see it.

Forget the future

The future comes soon enough without worrying about it, so don't let anxieties about tomorrow stop you getting on with your life today.

Most of us are brought up to think of the future and to work towards it. This is fine as long as you continue living to the fullest today. Being anxious about what the future holds is a waste of time. So, unless you're an alien with supernatural powers, you may as well accept that you can't control the future.

It's very handy, of course, to immerse yourself in the future when you want to avoid the fact that you're doing nothing in the present.

At other times, the notion of change (and changes are a natural part of the future) causes insecurities that stop us making choices. These insecurities leave us in a strange limbo for years, until we realise that resisting change (the future) is useless, and fighting it worse. Accept that we (with the help of our self-esteem) can survive anything, and we'll soon lose our fears about the future.

The trick to living in the present is to learn from your past mistakes, forgive yourself and then get on with enjoying your life.

Find your pen and paper and quickly write down all the things you worry about. How many of these worries are within your control? Cross out the ones that you have no direct control over.

You are now left with those items that you can do something about, so why aren't you? Doing something sure beats worrying. If you're not really motivated to find a promising solution for a nagging problem, was the problem really worth worrying about at all? Makes you wonder, doesn't it?

'Should' is a six-letter word

Life is a drag when you feel that you're letting yourself down (or others are letting you down) by not meeting your expectations. There's nothing wrong with having high hopes, but you can't expect perfection from anyone or anything.

So how do you know when you have set yourself 'perfection' as a goal? When you start your goal statements with the word 'should': "I should be able to pass this exam", "I should be able to get a boyfriend" or "I shouldn't have been so mean."

'Should' implies that you're disappointed with yourself – that you're a bit of a let-down. It's a negative word that is loaded with messages of guilt and blame.

This is how that six-letter word works:
"I should have done my homework, and because

I didn't I've let myself down (blame, blame) and I'm a truly rotten individual (guilt, guilt)." If you want to knock your self-esteem, then use the word 'should'.

From now on drop all the 'shoulds' from your life. Instead, look carefully at the demands you're making on yourself. Are they realistic? Are they really worth going for? Deciding that something is simply not worth the effort doesn't mean you've failed. It means that the goal wasn't so important after all.

Accept yourself as you are this very minute. So, okay you haven't finished your homework, but you will. You were rotten to that new kid today, but you'll apologise. It takes heaps of effort and involves lots of pain being horrible to yourself. On the other hand, it's so easy to be nice.

The ripple effect

Improved self-esteem will change your world, which in turn will affect everyone around you. Situations that you once found hard going will become easier; grouches who used to get you down will float past you. The ripple effect of self-respect just keeps on going. It knows no bounds and never runs out of steam, as the following shows:

When you respect yourself you:	Result:
Don't judge yourself.	You won't judge others.
Act kindly.	Others will act kindly to you.
Are open.	You'll get honesty in return.
Let people do things for you.	You'll realise you're worth it.
Are calm and relaxed.	No-one will wind you up.
Are patient with yourself.	You won't get angry and do self-destructive things.
Believe in yourself.	You won't need outside approval.
Accept that you'll make mistakes.	You won't be crushed when they occur.
Boost your confidence.	Your life will change.
Accept you are lovable.	People will love you.

Life is not a race, a contest or a competition. You don't have to do battle with anyone, nor compare yourself to others. You also don't have to go crazy when things go wrong. This is life, it comes with ups and downs and there's nothing you can do about it. You can, however, make it easier for yourself by being respectful of who and what you are. It's time to be friends with a very special person. **You**.

Resources

If you need further information or advice about the issues covered in this book, contact one of the organisations listed below.

Acne Support Group
www.stopspots.org
Tel: 0870 870 2263

Child and Adolescent Mental Health Services
www.camhs.net/yp/ki_self_esteem.asp

Healthy Eating
www.healthyeating.net

National Self-Harm Network
www.helen.ukpet.com/index.html
Tel: 0117 925 1119

Sexwise Confidential Advice Line
Tel: 0800 282930

The Site
www.thesite.org
Provides advice on confidence.

Uncommon Knowledge
www.uncommon-knowledge.co.uk/low_self_esteem

Index